Zohra's Ladder

And Other Moroccan Tales

by Pamela Windo

eye books

Challenging the way we see things

This Eye Classics edition first published in Great Britain in 2011, by:
Eye Books
7 Peacock Yard
Iliffe Street
London
SE17 3LH
www.eye-books.com

First published in Great Britain in 2005

Cover design by Emily Atkins/Jim Shannon
Text layout by Helen Steer

British Library Cataloguing in Publication Data
A catalogue record for this book is available from the British Library

The paperback edition of this book is printed in Poland.

ISBN: 978-1-903070-68-0

In memory of my parents, who always let me go.

Contents

PROLOGUE

L andscape, or its absence, is the setting for our lives. I was born and lived my first years in the rolling green country of southern England. These days, I live among the grey concrete forests of New York City. At the two most poignant moments of my life – at seventeen and at fifty – it was North Africa that claimed me. In spite of being a child who my mother said was born asking why, I have never dwelled on the reason my path took me there for such epiphanies. I accepted that it was too mysterious a concept to be answered rationally. Some have said it is my spiritual home.

Between Tunisia and Morocco, I spent more than ten years, by my own choice, living among people of different races, faiths, traditions and thoughts. My life in both countries was linked to a man. I went to Tunisia at the invitation of a young student I met in London and lived with him and his family for three years. Morocco happened seemingly by accident: it was to be my escape from love, somewhere to be alone and write. It was while living there that I met a man who changed the course of my life. How much did I take in of my life and travels; how much did I forget or reject? We live mostly oblivious of the changes in ourselves. Perhaps only now can I finally feel those changes.

When I began to write about Morocco, I realized that the more I tried to describe it, the more facts and explanations could not capture the country's essence. Mystery and mysticism lie beyond what the eye can see, in the deeper reaches of the heart. Our habit of analysing

7

everything has left us an un-mysterious people fearful of, yet still searching for, mystery. And so, I simply allowed those moments that wanted to be written to jump out at me.

The resulting stories are fragments in a kaleidoscope. Some of the moments I describe are light, others dark. As we love blue sky and sunshine, green fields, wide rivers and oceans, we also love dark night with its endless star-filled firmament. We love unforgiving mountains that reach up to heaven like cathedrals, and we love the emptiness and silence of the desert. The light and dark, the full and empty, both feed our souls.

Speaking of Morocco immediately conjures thoughts of mystery and intrigue, of sunlight and sensuality, of exotic handicrafts to decorate our homes, and of a refined and aromatic cuisine. All these are true, in abundance.

I first stepped foot in North Africa, in Tunis, when I was eighteen and, although my experiences stayed with me, they always felt more like a dream than reality. Half a lifetime later, I found myself back in North Africa, this time in Morocco. I had been living in New York, a British expatriate, and had begun to write. In my search for the ideal place, an escape from the familiar and from mundane distractions, I first chose a Greek island. But then I met two Moroccan brothers, Mustapha and Abdellah, who, with a mixture of pride and homesickness, urged me to visit their country instead. They even offered me the use of a small villa owned by their elder brother, Najib, that stood on the seawall of a fishing village called Asilah, not far from Tangiers.

I set off firmly believing I would stay put for three months and write. I had no plans to travel, had read nothing about the country and had no guidebook. On arriving by ferry, Najib greeted me with the news that the villa was no longer available – a sick friend was convalescing there. Instead, he took me first to his family's home in Casablanca and then on to Marrakesh, to stay in his mother-in-law's house. Fatima took me in as one of the family so that I began my life in Morocco on the inside, not as a tourist. The month I spent with her set me on the right course, initiating me into many aspects of the culture and giving me the courage to travel and live on my own. In doing so, I came face-to-face with people from all walks of life and experienced many vivid and unforgettable moments. By the time the three months ended, I had decided I would live in Marrakesh.

During the seven years I stayed, I came to understand why the experiences of my youth had seemed like a dream. In North Africa, life is lived in a sensuous now, in which the past cohabits indivisibly with the present, and the future holds little significance. The opposites of life go hand in hand at every turn: poverty and opulence, beauty and ugliness, clarity and ambiguity, light and shadow, the ancient and the modern. The traveller finds himself in a vivid yet dreamlike present. In yielding to this, life finds us. This is the mystery of Morocco.

An Afternoon at the Hammam

It was March, the end of my first week in Morocco. The air was damp, and I was chilled to the bone because after the first few days of hot sunshine, the spring rains had come and hadn't stopped for four whole days. Disappointed that I couldn't go out to explore Marrakesh, I lay curled up under a blanket in my little room off the courtyard, listening to the monotonous rhythmic splashing on the ceramic tiles. Fatima had offered me a larger room with stained-glass windows on the upper floor, but I'd preferred to stay in the courtyard, in the heart of the house, to observe the comings and goings.

Fatima lived deep within the massive ramparts, in the labyrinth of the Medina. Najib had accompanied me, as he doubted I'd ever find the house on my own. A 'petit taxi' dropped us as close as it could get to a narrow sandy alley, lined on either side with high, salmon-pink, windowless walls. It was hard to imagine that homes lay behind them; the only signs of this were the doors, low and solid, with great iron hinges, knockers and bolts. The walls protect the inner life as veils protect the features of the face. We wove our way along the teeming thoroughfare among women in rainbow-coloured djellabas, men in sombre turbans, boisterous children, mopeds, mules and bicycles. The sun beat down, intensifying everything, casting dark shadows beside brilliant bursts of sunlight, and the heady scents of musk, amber and incense mingled with the stench of animal and vegetable waste.

We stopped at a door, and Najib rapped loudly. A young girl about ten years old wearing an apron led us through a cool, dark passageway that brought us suddenly into a wide, sun-drenched courtyard. At its centre stood a marble fountain surrounded by bitter orange and lemon trees, and above it was a broad square of dazzling blue sky, framed by luminous sea-green roof tiles. It was an elegant old house – perhaps a hundred years old or more – and in need of repair, but the electric-blue doors, arabesque window grilles, whitewashed walls and colourful ceramic tiles shone with freshness and gave it an aura of timelessness. I had stepped out of reality into a dream. I fell in love with Morocco in that moment.

Fatima had been widowed some ten years before and had two sons and two daughters, all of them grown up and living away from home. She lived alone now, with a young orphan girl she'd taken in to train as a maid. An Arab from Fès, known for its fair-skinned people, Fatima was a small and delicate woman with short, wavy chestnut hair. She wore layers of pink gauze and reminded me of Bette Davis, having a similar petulant look about her eyes and mouth.

Now, suddenly, the door of my room opened wide. It was Fatima. "Toi veux aller hammam?" she asked in broken French, grinning shyly at me. She was offering to take me to the communal baths. Not only did the house have no heating, there was no hot water either. The thought of steaming and soaking for hours sounded like heaven. Poor heat- and air-conditioned brat, I admitted to myself, sitting up quickly and nodding to my thoughtful host.

While I got dressed, Fatima busied herself with gathering buckets, pots, towels and sundry items from a storeroom in the courtyard, and before we left the house, she handed me a djellaba to wear, arranging the hood deeply over my forehead, like her own. We scurried along the crowded kerbs, muddy and waterlogged from all the rain, looking like monks in our all-concealing habits. We passed the local mosque, tucked between two grocers' stalls; a Muslim has to eat to live and be clean to pray. *Passage interdit aux non-Musulmans*, a sign read: entry forbidden to non-Muslims. This was the result of French soldiers' misuse of the baths during the Protection. And then we came to the neighbourhood hammam, with its two blue-tiled doorways set in rough ochre walls. Above them, two caricatured faces, primitively painted like graffiti, signalled the separate entrances for men and women – a veiled woman with black, slanting eyes and a turbaned man with a pointed black beard. I followed Fatima through a low door, swishing a striped curtain aside, into a bare, dimly lit changing room. A clutch of women wearing headscarves squatted as they brewed mint tea over a charcoal burner that gave off warm woody fumes. Fatima told me the women are called tayebas, which means cooks, because they fetch and carry water and scrub the pregnant, the rich or the lazy. I immediately felt their sharp eyes scrutinizing me and imagined their sharp tongues discussing me too, as they gossiped in their singsong medley of Berber and Arabic, perhaps laying odds on how long I'd last in the heat.

Fatima and I undressed down to our panties. It was a shock to see all the other women lolling about in various stages of undress, before or after bathing – unashamed and unselfconscious compared to the extreme modesty of their clothes and behaviour in the street. We left our belongings in open cubby-holes and picked up our buckets. A heavy wooden door, sodden with years of steam, led into the hammam rooms. Inside, it was swelteringly hot, and the first glimpse was a bit daunting. In the ghostly steam and half-light, all I could see was bare flesh, dark faces with dark eyes, and dark, wet hair. Why in an unfamiliar situation do we fear the worst? For me, it was the shock of such uninhibited physical intimacy, as well as the thought of all that communal dirt.

When I had grown accustomed to the semi-darkness, I noticed naked women coating their bodies with saboon bildi, a thick, dark-brown jelly-like soap that looked suspiciously like engine grease but was made from olive-pressing residue. Others had red masks on their faces, a skin tonic that dripped blood-like streaks down their shoulders into the streams of swirling water. Frothing soapsuds floated everywhere, and the peel from oranges eaten as snacks littered the floor. We stepped arch by arch through the steam-filled rooms, each one darker and steamier than the one before. The only light came from a small, round skylight in the central room's domed ceiling. I slipped once or twice on the hot and wet tiled floor as I picked my way through voluptuously curved ladies, pendant-breasted matrons, sleek young women and brown-limbed children yelling their indignation at being so thoroughly scrubbed and soaped. A sea of inscrutable dark eyes registered my presence: I was the only woman with blond hair and blue eyes, and my otherwise fashionable thinness seemed suddenly boyish and unwomanly. I wondered if they resented my invasion of their private territory, but when I smiled, they smiled back and I understood it was up to me, the outsider, to bridge the gap.

In the third and last room, the hottest and steamiest, Fatima stopped to fill one of our buckets. She rinsed an area of tiles, threw down a rubber mat and pointed at it. I sat down obediently. The women in this room were plying to and fro, filling buckets at the gushing water taps, and the pleasant smell of olive and lemon soap hung in the steam-drenched air. There was so much hot water flowing everywhere, I forgot my fears about the hammam's cleanliness and leaned back against the tiled wall to soak up the steam and let my pores open. Everything was slow and methodical, with a meditative concentration on getting your body clean. The woman next to me was going through a precise set of motions that Fatima explained was the Muslim's ritual ablution before prayer. It was Thursday; everyone was getting clean for Friday, Holy Day.

After a while, we got up and set our four buckets in the line by the taps. When we had filled them, we returned to our spot and set them all around us: three with near-boiling water and one with cold, for mixing. Fatima handed me a blob of the brown soap with a gesture that meant I should spread it all over me. We left it for a quarter of an hour, and then rinsed it off. Fatima pressed her hand against my shoulder and motioned me to lie down. I stretched out on the baking-hot tiles, my head resting against her thighs, while she slowly scrubbed me with a coarse black mitt called a keess, limb by limb, over and over, until my skin was almost sore, flushed pink and tingling. Rolls of dead skin littered my body; it was hard to believe how dirty I'd been. When she had finished scrubbing, she poured water all over me to swill away the grey debris.

While Fatima turned her efforts on herself, I became aware of a little boy about three years old standing motionless a few feet away. He was staring at me with wide brown eyes, as if mesmerized, his little penis pointing stiffly upwards. He must have seen many naked women in the hammam, and I wondered what effect that would have on him; as he grew up, would he be more, or less, fascinated by the female of the species? Thinking it would probably be more, I turned my body aside. As I did so, a wrinkled old woman tapped my arm; her chin was dotted with a faded, inky tattoo, her smile decorated with a set of pink, almost toothless gums. She waved one mitted hand in the air, placed the other firmly on my back and began to scrub. For a moment, I felt affronted by her impudence, but when her twinkling eyes met mine she reminded me of my grandmother, so I let her carry on scrubbing. I had never been naked with my mother or my sister, let alone my grandmother, yet here I was, comfortable with complete strangers.

The last part of the bathing ritual was the application of sludgy clay paste to my hair. To rinse it off required me to bend my head between my open legs, a job another old matron gleefully assigned herself to. The washing of the thin, pale foreigner had become the afternoon's entertainment. She gave me a wide-toothed comb, and as I worked through the long strands, she poured pot after pot of water that streamed from my crown over my shoulders and down my back and felt like a healing river. I was by then utterly lost in sensuality; my body felt transparent and my hair like silk.

I had lost all sense of time when I tipped the last bowl of water over my head. I wasn't looking forward to leaving this warm, intimate world of women and returning to the muddy streets, the rain, and the cold house. We took our time in the changing room, where I sat on a slatted bench with a towel wound round my steaming body. I'd never been so clean. When I stood up to dress, I caught sight of myself in a small cracked mirror and barely recognized my face: I was a glowing brilliant pink with eyes that shone like beacons. When I told Fatima I felt like a new person, she laughed with delight and told the ladies of the hammam who were busy inspecting me. They laughed loudly too, waving their hennaed hands at me in approval. But I was more interested in what Fatima was thinking about me. How could she know how much this initiation had touched me? It had felt like a long-lost celebration I had deeply missed.

The hammam was a communal baptism, washing away more than

dirt. There'd been helping hands in the darkness, limbs touching and eyes meeting, and I understood why the women spent hours there in each other's company. I felt regret for what we more 'liberated' women seem to have lost, in doing and thinking like men. Unlike us, the women I saw were together asserting and rejoicing in their difference from men, and in that I saw their strength.

RABIAH'S HOUSE

When Rabiah and I left her apartment in Casablanca and set off for the bus station, she was dressed in her deepest travelling disguise: a steel-grey, ankle-length djellaba, its hood folded severely across her forehead, and a matching grey muslin ngeb that stretched across her face and left only a slit for her deep-set, kohl-lined eyes. My travelling outfit was more practical: blue jeans and a leather jacket, and my hair was loose.

Rabiah was Najib's mother, a Soussi Berber from the south of Morocco. Like Fatima, she was widowed young, but in her case, she had been left with eight children – four sons and four daughters – to bring up alone. To better educate her brood, she had moved from her mud house in the Anti Atlas Mountains to an apartment in cosmopolitan Casablanca. Sturdily built with broad shoulders, she had a strong, sculpted face and shiny tawny-olive complexion. From the moment I met her, between her stoical expression and austere clothes, I found her quite frightening.

After I had been living with Fatima in Marrakesh for about a month, Rabiah had offered me the use of a small family house in Agadir, on Morocco's southern Atlantic coast. I had accepted immediately, eager to see more of the country and to live alone, anonymously, among its people. At the last minute, Rabiah insisted on accompanying me to prepare the house for my stay, although I rather got the impression it was an excuse to take a well-deserved break.

The bus left around ten o'clock in the evening with me the only foreigner on board and would arrive in Agadir, Insh'allah, around six the next morning. We were making the trip at night because it was Ramadan – the month when Muslims fast from dawn to sunset – so Rabiah could eat and drink on the way. We sat side by side in silence, getting a good deal of stares from the other passengers. From time to time, Rabiah cast an authoritative glance my way that made me feel like her ward, although there could only have been a few years' difference in our age. "Toi fait harira demain," she said quite suddenly, breaking her icy countenance with the hint of a grin: your turn to cook the soup tomorrow. She meant the traditional soup of Ramadan. I laughed in surprise but answered the challenge by reciting a list of the ingredients I'd seen Fatima use, hesitating for the last item.

From the seat behind me, a young man's voice cued me: "Hummus" – chick-peas. As I turned round to thank the owner of the voice, I noticed that Rabiah's eyes were twinkling and her white teeth were glinting beneath the ngeb; she was shaking with silent laughter. After years of being camouflaged by veils and djellabas, she had become expert in expressing herself with her dark eyes and hennaed hands, the only parts of her body left visible and free. When I turned around again to ask the man if he knew how to cook the soup, to be friendly, I felt a sharp pinch on my thigh. I jumped and looked at Rabiah. She simply shook her head at me, and with that, I began to understand what it was like to have a strict Muslim mother.

The bus passed through the noisy, brightly illuminated metropolis and the interminable sprawling suburbs, and then the darkened countryside took over, and we were scuttling across the Chaouia plains with only the faint lights of a small village here and there to relieve the darkness. At one point, noticing my purse on my knees, Rabiah secured its straps around the armrest, in case of 'voleurs,' she warned, as if I had been careless. Satisfied everything was ship-shape, she produced a jar of orange juice from her bulging travelling bag. "Tiens, Madame," she said, offering me a cup and maintaining the formality.

"Chokran," I answered. Communication between us amounted to very few words; hand signals and facial gestures were our vocabulary. Sometimes I thought I detected a spark of adventure in her eyes. Travel has a way of bringing things out in people you might not otherwise see, and I wondered if she found me as interesting to watch as I found her.

As the night grew rapidly colder, I covered myself with my coat. One of the male passengers had an interminable, ear-shattering fit of sneezes, and then finally darkness and silence reigned as everyone fell asleep. Before dozing off, it occurred to me to check where the bus toilet was. I looked to the back but there was no sign of one. When I whispered this to Rabiah, she simply muttered, "Agadir." It seemed impossible that she could wait until we arrived, so I assumed we'd stop somewhere on the way.

Around one o'clock, I awoke with a start as the bus pulled out of the blackness and stopped at a roadside café. It was bustling with life, all lit up by dozens of flickering gas and kerosene lamps. Outside, vendors with carts of oranges, apples and midget bananas barked their prices, but tables and warmth drew the passengers inside. As I stepped down from the bus, the hot smells of roasting meat roused me as they wafted across in the clouds of smoke billowing from a series of charcoal braziers lined with skewers of beef and lamb. Next to these were cauldrons of oil filled with sizzling pommes frites, and blackened kettles spewing steam.

Rabiah refused to go inside the café because it was full of men, so I went on in alone, keen to eat and drink and get warm. I found myself among a throng of swarthy countrymen dressed in threadbare burnooses, haggard from the day's hard labour and fasting. I noticed their eyes flash in my direction – a quick sizing-up that contained no trace of hostility – but after that, they paid me no more attention, returning to their hearty eating, smoking and talking. I wondered which man had a wife at home, which did his duty and which one cherished his wife? I thought that, unlike us, their concept of love must be a fleeting dream, and I felt a moment's shameful privilege. There was no sign of beer or alcohol; I'd not seen or drunk a drop since I'd arrived in Morocco. Poverty, dirt and dust, and the endless fight against them were evident and palpable. But in spite of the harsh edge of life, I felt celebration in the air.

I bought some 'frites' served in a paper cone with a dollop of mustard, and a glass of sweet dark-brewed tea crammed full of fresh mint leaves. Together, they came to the equivalent of fifty cents.

I took them outside where I found Rabiah stalking around in the shadows chewing on an apple. She looked at my snack. "Sh'hal?" She had asked how much I'd paid. Upon hearing the amount, she shook her finger. "Bezzef!" Too much, she said. Her budget defied reason, but then I thought of her eight children and understood why.

Before I'd finished eating, a scruffy boy with shaved head and bare feet ran up to me and pointed to my food and at his mouth. I handed him the last of the frites just as a second boy ran out, at which the first boy snatched the cone and stuffed the frites into his mouth in one go, until it bulged and there was no room left to chew. It was a harrowing image that took me unawares, and one that I would not easily forget.

After this, I set off self-consciously towards the café's toilet. The stall marked 'Dames' had only a half door that displayed one's head and feet. Beside it, a bearded and turbaned man was washing and spitting loudly into a dirt-stained sink. A waiter noticed my hesitation and gallantly shooed the man away with loud reprimands. It was a squatting lavatory, a crude hole in the ground; the sight and stench got me quickly out of there. No wonder Rabiah had trained herself to do without.

Back in the bus, on our way again, I slept in fits and starts, my legs soon stiff from the damp and pervasive cold. At one point, Rabiah gave me another of her pinches and pointed ahead to the High Atlas Mountains that loomed dark and ominous across the southern horizon, and to a hazy half-moon perched between two peaks.

Hours later, in the midst of a fitful doze, the ever-watchful Rabiah nudged me yet again. It was daybreak, and we were hurtling through a mountain ridge on a narrow curved road, approaching the Atlantic Ocean. Finally, the bus pulled up at the terminus. The morning was clear and warm as Rabiah waved down an orange 'petit taxi' that drove us through the empty, slowly waking seaside town. We arrived at the 'quartier industriel,' where I could see no apparent signs of industry, and turned into a small dusty square in the middle of which a lone palm tree stood sentinel, its trunk overtaken by mauve clematis in profuse flower.

The taxi stopped at a brown door set in a plain cement wall. Beside it, a large number '5' had been daubed. The house stood in a quiet street of flat-roofed, whitewashed dwellings, a few blocks from the beach. I couldn't help noticing the house had no roof, and the street wall could easily be scaled with a ladder. But if it were safe enough for Rabiah, I reasoned, it would be safe enough for me. The door opened – with some difficulty, because the key was quite rusted – into a small tiled courtyard filled with pots of marigolds and mint and troughs of overgrown succulents. On each of the courtyard's three walls was a brown door: one opened into a small kitchen, another into a rectangular blue and white salon, and the last into a simple windowless living room.

Clearly, the house hadn't been lived in for some while; sand and dust had blown into every corner and crevice. Without stopping to rest, Rabiah set to work. She began by opening the shutters and doors, then rolled up her sleeves, tucked her skirts into her pantaloons, took off her sandals and filled some buckets with water from the courtyard tap. I was tired and would rather have slept or wandered off to the beach. But it was Ramadan, and I should be more respectful. I certainly couldn't allow my host to think I was lazy, and so with the help of the fresh sea air and the morning sunshine, I rallied and rolled up my sleeves to help.

Our first job was to clean the kitchen, bare except for cupboards and a sink, and without refrigerator or water heater. After washing and scrubbing it, we turned our attention to the salon and living room, shaking the divan covers and blankets and then hanging them on the clothes line to air. Then we threw buckets of water all round the courtyard, wading barefoot as we swilled away the dirt. Rabiah watered and weeded the pots of flowers, uprooting one overgrown plant in spite of my pleas for mercy, and drastically pruned a cactus that had spread its tentacles too far for her liking. Finally, she nodded towards the shower-cum-toilet cubicle set on the far side of the courtyard. "Pour toi, mettre sabon et shampooing," she said, pointing to a narrow wooden shelf, speaking her first words since we'd arrived. It was a kind gesture, designed to make me feel at home, and with it, I felt a rush of unexpected affection. When I placed my jars and creams, matching pink towel and face cloth on the shelf, they looked absurdly out of place in the concrete cubicle that had only a towel hook, a tin shower nozzle and a plastic bucket.

Rabiah stopped and looked all round: she had transformed the house into a seaside chalet, the kind of place I had dreamed of. Satisfied with her work, she went off to wash and then to pray in the living room. I took the opportunity to arrange my belongings in the salon she had suggested I use as my bedroom. Its door opened wide onto the courtyard, as did the shuttered windows, so that I could see blue sky wherever I looked. I would be living almost entirely in the open air.

When Rabiah had finished her prostrations, she came to join me. "Nimshiu hanout, toi mange." Let's go to the grocer; you must eat, she had said, although she herself could not eat until sundown. A few doors up the street, there was a ramshackle store, a kind of recess in the wall, with a counter giving onto the street and a battered steel shutter to close it. The grocer wore a blue overall and a white crocheted skullcap, and was playing checkers with another man on a hand-drawn scrap of cardboard, so engrossed in the game it took him a few moments to notice we were waiting. Basic goods were arranged and toppling on narrow shelves, with only one brand of anything, in miniature sample-type sizes. Rabiah bought a litre of milk in a sealed plastic bag, a round loaf of bread, two eggs, a few ounces of butter and coffee, and a solid lump of off-white sugar, all of which the grocer wrapped in bits of white paper. The breakfast she made for me from these ingredients was delicious and certainly welcome after the journey and the work, although I ate with some misgivings knowing she was fasting. Meanwhile, Rabiah gave me no reason to think I too ought to fast.

Before I had finished, two women neighbours came to visit. They knew Rabiah was in town because one of them, the proud owner of a telephone, had received a call from Najib to ask if we'd arrived safely. I thought how easily I had become used to living without a telephone; I had only made two calls in the month I'd been in Morocco. Although the women spoke in the fast Soussi Berber tongue, of which I understood not one word, the singsong sound of their voices mixed with the language of their hands and faces were eloquent enough to satisfy my curiosity and imagination. Their eyes met mine often, looking straight into them, and their hands moved constantly to touch me as they talked. It was clear that neither of the women was well off, nor were they outwardly beautiful, but both possessed grace and dignity that lent them another kind of beauty, one that came, I thought, with the owning of oneself completely, for better or worse. In spite of their circumstances, I felt they were not at odds with themselves.

Fadma was of medium height and lean-boned; I guessed her to be in her sixties. Her deeply-lined skin was pale-olive, her laughing eyes faded hazel-brown. When she spoke, her low resonant voice, like her eyes, was full of whimsy. But I was most intrigued with her clothes, and stared with envy to see how she had achieved such simple elegance: a crisp, long, green and white spotted sleeveless shift they call a pajama worn over a white and green under-bodice, a woven black belt at her waist and a maroon cardigan on top. But it was with her veil that her creativity excelled: Fadma had swirled around her shoulders, neck and head a sheath of white muslin with green embroidered borders, its final flourish hanging capriciously from the right side of her head. The finishing touches were three rows of jet beads around her wrinkled neck, at her wrist a beaten silver bracelet, and on her fingers silver rings worn thin with work and time.

The other woman was pretty and petite, somewhat younger; her name was Sfia. She was swathed in a thick, ivory wool hayk that left only her face visible. Her black eyes were limpid, her complexion smooth like amber. When she laughed, which she did constantly, she blithely revealed herself the owner of just three tall, crooked teeth. Perhaps it was a shame her beauty was marred, but I thought her acceptance of herself made pity irrelevant: I saw her living a life in which she accepted that nothing was perfect, and in which value was given to more intrinsic things. There was always a reason to laugh, her eyes told the world, in spite of hardship or having few teeth. When I asked to photograph them both, they covered themselves completely with their veils, leaving just a peephole to see through. I clicked the camera anyway, capturing nothing but two ghostly white forms.

When the women left it was time to go shopping for provisions in the souk. Rabiah and I set off along streets of sand, debris and poverty at the back of town. But there were moments of beauty too: a solitary jacaranda tree on a derelict plot of land, its blossoms drifting down to form a soft mauve carpet on the ground; an ornate blue door set in a crumbling earthen wall. Most of all, I noticed the contrasts between the people: a little boy in shorts dutifully leading an old man in turban and flowing robes across the street, a teenage girl with wild tresses and short skirt beside her mother, entirely concealed by her garments. At one point, Rabiah recognized a man, though he didn't at first recognize her. You had obviously to remember small details about a woman: her posture, the shape of her feet and hands, even her shoes. She allowed the man only one glimpse into her eyes, then talked to him standing sideways. But before my own eyes, I saw her transformed into a shy, fluttering woman; the presence of a man had brought out her feminine side. I had the feeling she enjoyed my witnessing the moment.

A ten-minute walk brought us to a crumbling arch in a high, orange-washed mud wall the length of two or three city blocks. Inside was a vast enclosure, the largest weekly souk in Morocco, jam-packed with people and produce. At the far end, the Anti Atlas peaks hung imperiously above the wild scene. As far as the eye could see, it was a seething mass of tilting makeshift tents and lean-tos with slanting poles; of farmers coming and going, shouting and bargaining; and of donkeys, mules and laden carts being dragged this way and that. It was an orgy of freshness, of eye-popping colours and pungent, organic smells. All the vegetables seemed to have come from well-loved gardens, unlike the limp selection in my supermarket at home.

My senses were so overwhelmed and I was so distracted by everything, I suddenly realized Rabiah was no longer at my side. I searched for her among the hundreds of hooded female forms until I picked out the steel-grey robe beside sculpted pyramids of yellow, red and orange spices. I walked over to join her and she grabbed my arm as if I was an errant child, moving me on to the olive stalls set against the market walls. There, she bought some of the spicy green and small black oil-cured olives from one of the merchants, a lively old man who constantly rearranged his bowls of glossy black, green and pinkish-brown fruit. I waited less enthusiastically while she bought meat; the stalls reeked of flesh and blood and were a gory sight. Sheep heads still bearing their horns hung on huge hooks, carcasses were spread out on wooden slabs still bearing testicles and beside them lay cloven hooves and tripe. I preferred not to imagine what dishes were prepared from such things, and was relieved when Rabiah bought a simple lamb shank, arguing fiercely with the butcher about a few cents in the price. Finally, she was satisfied we had everything we needed and I took one handle of the heavy basket as we walked back home.

Ftour – the meal that breaks the fast – had to be ready by sunset, at seven, and it was already past six. I watched keenly everything Rabiah did as she moved deftly from task to task, squatting and working on the clean tiles of the kitchen floor. On a single burner over a small gas cylinder, she warmed the harira soup that Sfia had brought us: boiled eggs and prepared coffee with steamed milk and wild thyme that smelled so delicious I wondered how I'd ever wait to taste it. Under her critical eye, I began to help but immediately sensed that if things weren't done her way, they weren't done right. It was not the time or place to point out that there were other ways to do things. In no time at all, the flour was ready and the lamb tajine for our dinner later set over the embers of a charcoal fire in the courtyard.

As dusk fell around us, the house filled with warm aromas that brought home how ravenous I was. After setting a rush mat on the courtyard tiles and bowls and utensils on a small round table, Rabiah finally sat down. We were two women, one dark, one fair – a world apart in every way except that we were both mothers – waiting to hear the call that signalled the fast was over. When the muezzin filled the evening sky with their loud wailing chants, we said 'Bismillah' – thanks to Allah – and ate the first date, an age-old ritual from the desert, followed by spoonfuls of the thick harira soup. Afterwards, the sweet, aromatic coffee proved to be the best I'd ever tasted. Rabiah ate fast and with great appetite: the preparation of food is slow and precise, the eating swift and decisive. You are hungry, there is food; always give thanks. I had learned by then that to slurp indicated the food was good, to belch meant you were full and satisfied. Rabiah did both and I heartily followed suit. After the meal, we washed the dishes in cold water with a paste made of Tide powder, listening to Berber music on an old transistor radio. It was clear from her smile that Rabiah took pleasure in us doing the chore together.

Just as we finished, Fadma's two young daughters Hafida and Fatima came to visit, giggling a lot and eyeing me up and down. They were both in their early twenties with mops of jet-black, curly hair. Where Hafida had light olive skin and was full-bodied and extrovert, her sister Fatima was darker skinned, sleek and delicate. Moroccans are all polyglots, and even the sisters spoke in a constantly changing mix of Berber, Moroccan Arabic, with some French thrown in for my benefit. They asked me about America, about work and money, but omitted the more pressing subjects of men, love and sex in Rabiah's presence. They teased me too about the frozen and fast foods we eat and how we use metal instruments to eat with and constantly analyze our food, as if we were in a laboratory. "Tomorrow you do Ramadan all day, don't eat nothing!" Hafida challenged me – a playful reminder that this foreign woman must also experience hunger.

"Okay," I said, laughing with them, at which Hafida leaned over to whisper something to her sister. They giggled, and then Hafida invited me to go with them for their ritual Ramadan walk along the beach promenade. I asked how come they could go out alone. She explained that although it was not usually permitted that any girl or woman, let alone an unmarried one, go out anywhere without a male relative or female chaperone, Ramadan allowed them a brief reprieve: it was the custom then to take an evening stroll, to see and be seen by the local young men without censuring eyes upon them. This happened, she added, only in the more modern towns and cities.

"If you give me a djellaba," I replied, thinking it would help me blend in and not be stared at. Hafida smacked her hands and ran off home. I slipped the plum-red robe she brought me over my jeans, covering my hair with the deep, pointed hood. The girls gazed at me as if seeing a different person, or as if in me they suddenly saw themselves in a different light. Rabiah's lips broke into a reluctant smile of approval as the three of us set off down the street.

During my days exploring Marrakesh, I had lost some of my self-consciousness at being a lone foreign woman. I was at ease with the girls, and, although they could have been my daughters, as we walked and talked and joked together, the difference in our ages faded away. I felt young again. Or perhaps being with Rabiah had something to do with it. One young man called out playfully: "C'est ta cousine?" clearly seeing through my disguise but grasping its purpose.

"Yes, how you find her?" Hafida retorted brazenly, then turned to me. "It's your eyes, no Moroccan has eyes like yours," she said.

The promenade was unlit, except for the café lights and the moon's rays catching the crests of the silver surf, and was packed solid with shadowy forms. The three of us were shoulder to shoulder in a swelling sea of dark-haired and dark-skinned young men and women. Even in the darkness, I could see their eyes darting back and forth, searching among the crowd for a sweetheart, for a husband or wife. I could feel the longing from their separate, guarded worlds, and sensed the girls' thinly disguised hope of finding the one tonight. But since only an ill-bred girl would approach a man, I asked how the one would approach her. Hafida explained that if a man were attracted and he didn't know her family, he would have to follow her or her friends and ask questions in the neighbourhood. If he were brave enough, he might approach her himself to ask where she lived. Then he would send a family member to meet her family.

The main event of the evening was to stop for coffee in one of the cafés. Two more dark and vivacious young girls came to join us, dressed like the sisters in brightly-coloured satin djellabas. Young women rarely wear the ngeb that older women like Rabiah still insist on wearing over their face. One of the girls with huge brown eyes leaned towards me immediately after we were introduced. "The women in America are strong, I think," she began, in heavily accented French. "And you can easily meet men," she quickly added, waiting for my reaction. The other girls sat back and listened intently. Without wanting to go too far, I tried diplomacy, saying there were always, everywhere, those who were strong and those who weren't, that things between men and women were simply different in America, not better. The girl who had asked the question was endearingly honest, her mind more focused on how she would behave when she found a man rather than on simply finding one. "But you're free. Why can't I work, and he work and we do things together, share the chores, why not?" she appealed to me. She told me her three sisters had found 'l'amour,' but said it with a mixture of envy and scepticism. At least they were married, she added, with children and a home. I could hear her wondering why she didn't have these things, and if she ever would.

After a few short-lived repartees with young men who passed close by the girls, it came time to go home, without any sign of a serious suitor. But, as Ramadan wasn't over yet, there was still time to hope. The earnest girl walked beside me. "A man I met, he tells me when I talk I am like a man. He like me first, then he leave," she said sadly. My heart ached for her, more than for the other girls who seemed not to be questioning. If I told her to be herself, regardless, would I be sealing a lonely fate for her? And if I told her to shut up in order to marry? Where and how would she meet her match? And why was she the only one to say these things?

I felt even more like a young girl when Rabiah opened the door and, with a half-frown put on for my benefit, said, "Dormir toi," – time to sleep. After a hurried wash in the Spartan cubicle, I went to bed at the end of a very long day that had begun in the bus the night before. In a day or so, when Rabiah left, I would be alone in the house. I had wanted a simple, solitary life, and soon I would have just that. My eyes began to close, but before I fell asleep, I heard the door to my room creak slightly. I didn't move as Rabiah crept over to tuck me in. When she had tiptoed out, I looked out of the window at the moon shining above the courtyard. Rabiah was a woman of great presence and power, with a generous and knowing heart. I would miss her.

Pilgrimages to the Post Office

My life was a dream come true. I'd been living in the house in Agadir for about a month, and the only thing missing was news from home. I'd written letters and postcards to everyone and went every other day to the post office, hoping to find their responses waiting for me. Each time, the clerk would go to the international mail cubbyhole and then come back, shaking his head. "Ma'keynsh," nothing, he'd say. I would frown and ask him to search again, but still nothing. And then I left Agadir to live in Marrakesh and filled out a form to have my mail forwarded.

And so it was to the main Gueliz post office in Marrakesh that I now made my daily pilgrimages for mail. A huge high-ceilinged place built by the French colonialists, the post office was always crowded and noisy, and a monumental challenge to my patience and temper. The half-dozen counter windows had signs indicating various services. But these were flagrantly ignored, partly because people couldn't read, but mainly because they had no concept - or desire - to make a line and wait in an orderly fashion. This meant that each window had a large amoebic mass swelling in front of it. Men and women, body to body, forgot the proscribed modesty in their blind urge to get whatever it was they were after, which wasn't mail, as far as I could tell.

I would go to the window marked Poste Restante (a notion that until then I'd thought very romantic) and at first stood at the back of the mass, among flailing arms and raised voices, thinking I'd move forward as the customers were served and left. Realizing the physics of the thing didn't work that way - that more people just came and muscled into the mass - I soon concluded the only way was to enter the mass and try to elbow and shoulder my way to the front. No one took offense, there were no shouts or insults; everyone accepted that fighting was the way to get there. The only exception that I saw was that ladies of a certain age would shove themselves right in front of the mostly male crowd, asserting the respect of womanhood and old age, which always got them served ahead of the men. After noticing this, I would shove a little harder.

The clerks were like sullen robots, having clearly given up trying to maintain order. One day, my patience worn thin, I suddenly raised my voice and said in my pidgin Arabic, "What, are we all animals here?" And in the moment of reverent silence that followed, and with the stunned surprise of the clerks, I signalled with my arms the direction of a line, which, to my astonishment, everyone shuffled to get into. But the phenomenon was short-lived; probably only for the duration of my presence that day. I had obviously scared them: it wasn't everyday a blonde foreign woman told them what to do.

On each visit to the Post Office, I was caught between shame at having to shove and seeing the funny side. If any of my family or friends could have seen me, they would have laughed themselves silly. Eventually, one day a few days after my birthday, the clerk finally handed me a large envelope. I was so overcome, I took it like a famished animal with its prey and sat down on the wall outside the post office to read it. The envelope contained a giant-size birthday card sent by colleagues from the office I had last worked at in New York. In moments, I was in a flood of tears: the card contained seven signatures with seven messages for a happy birthday. It was as if, after all that waiting, I'd won the lottery.

Weeks went by again without the clerk handing me any letters, although I knew my friends would have replied to mine. He would shake his head without even looking at me, as he knew me well by then. Had everyone forgotten me? No, the post office was taking them and hiding them, spying on me, I decided. One day, after the clerk had shaken his head yet again, I was so distraught I strode up the wide marble stairway at the far end of the post office to see the man who ran the place. In a corridor of brown walls and dark wood floors, there were several doors, all closed except one. I marched towards it, peered inside, and could see a man in a suit sitting at a large metal desk. I entered the office, went up to the desk and brought my fist down on it with a fierce thump that shocked me more than the man. Having got his undivided attention, I then, in my best French, told him I wasn't getting my mail and asked what was he intending to do about it?

"Madame," he said in a strained official voice, "Calmez-vous." And with that he got up. I followed him as he went down the marble stairs. He checked with the clerk, assuming a serious expression, and confirmed there was no mail for me. And with that he made a puckered grimace, raised his hands as if to say that was the end of the matter, and went back upstairs.

It wasn't until much later, I discovered that the envelope containing the seven postcards with the thank-you messages I'd written to each of my colleagues had arrived in their office in New York, opened and empty. I was right; the post office had been spying on me. Friends later told me too, they had written. Where the letters went I'll never know.

There were many things I had to resign myself to in Marrakesh; not getting mail was just one of them.

THE ADVENTUROUS
FRENCHMAN

The weeks passed slowly, timelessly, in Khadija's house. I stayed within the neighbourhood and absorbed its rhythm, spending part of each day visiting with Hafida, Fatima and their mother, Fadma. The beach that I had thought to spend my days at did not lure me away. Newspapers, television, restaurants and bars had no place in my life either, although in a town full of tourists they were readily available.

One morning, I found myself craving the company of a foreigner, or rather, the company of one of my own race. I walked to a seaside café where I chose a seat in the sun. The café was crowded with the pink and happy faces of tourists, and at a table in the shade of a leafy alcove, I noticed a man poring over a detailed map. His thick dark hair was greying, but he was still handsome, with a muscular body, self-assured and sexy. He glanced up at me from time to time. Clearly not a tourist, he intrigued me. Hazarding a guess he was French, I asked, "Vous allez où?" He gestured to the seat opposite, and when I sat down he turned the map around for me to see and pointed to a mountain range.

His name was Guy; he was planning a ten day hike in the High Atlas, accompanied by a local guide who would find him a bed and food each night in the Berbers' mud and straw homes. I was impressed when he showed me the difficult trail he would take, and asked if he would take me with him.

"It's too arduous," he answered quickly.

"I'm fit, and I don't mind dirt and hardship," I insisted. He smiled, but said it meant walking thirty miles a day, and with that dismissed my request. The trek was to begin the following morning and he seemed impatient, at a loss what to do until then.

"Will you take me to the waterfalls of Immouzer?" I asked. "I'll pay for the gas." He looked at his watch, thought for a moment, and then grinned and nodded.

In no time we were heading up the rugged coastline, into the seaward Anti Atlas Mountains. Conversation flowed easily. "I love Morocco; I used to live here. You see, I love a life of contrasts, of extremes; it's a challenge," he said, his eyes lit up. "And I like my mind so sharp and clear that nothing distracts me. And then afterwards, I love to let myself go and relax – with a whisky," he laughed.

Driving too fast, Guy navigated the steep twists and turns and roller-coaster ascents and descents, through barren sandstone ranges, past strange overhanging rock formations and isolated hamlets of gingerbread homes. I breathed a sigh of relief when we entered a verdant narrow valley cut into the rocks. A jungle of palm trees, pink oleander and green bamboo splurged around the anise-green water of a stream that ran over smooth curved rocks into limpid pools. Guy pulled the car over and we got out to rest, to absorb the peace. While Guy lay down and peered into the water, his nose almost touching it as he tried to catch a fish, I followed a frog as it leaped from pool to pool. There wasn't a sound except for the trickle of water and the songs of birds. Two English hikers had come upon this hidden oasis back in 1960 and had named it Paradise Valley. I imagined their delight at the discovery, and thought how right they had been to call it paradise.

Back on the road, we motored along hillsides spread with wild thyme, lavender and gorse, and with terraces of almond, argan and olive trees. The foaming white waterfalls appeared suddenly in the distance, tumbling between the dense green foliage of a pine forest. We parked near the falls and strolled along a pine-scented path among huge ominous boulders. I followed Guy until we reached the rock face above a deep turquoise blue pool into which the water fell. Without waiting for me, he scaled a steep slippery rock and then turned back to me. "Your hand!" he commanded, reaching out. I would never have attempted to do this alone, but I quickly found myself standing beside him, staring at the abyss below. The local youths put us both to shame, hurling their bodies down into the pool to earn a few dirhams from a small band of tourists standing nearby.

On our way back to the car, Guy hurried past a handful of locals hustling us to buy fossils, waving one aside with a gruff, "Saafi, enough!"

The man responded quickly, "A man who rushes is a man already dead!"

"He's right," Guy muttered, frowning. On the way back home, he soon forgot the man's comment and drove too fast again. I sat back, praying for our safety, concentrating on the gorgeous landscape as it passed before me a second time. When the rows of lights on the seaside promenade lit the horizon ahead of us, he asked if I'd join him for dinner at a restaurant.

There were soft banquettes, dimmed lights and attentive waiters. It felt good to relax after the long drive and enjoy the first glass of wine I'd tasted for months. I ate the fish tajine with my fingers and Guy smiled; he had only just noticed the dark henna designs marking the palms of my hands. His deep-set eyes were blue-grey, intense, and I knew he would eventually make a pass, the adventurer would not resist. When it came later at my door, it took him a moment or two to recover from my rejection, but then he smiled and wished me good luck as he drove away.

I woke early the following morning when Hafida brought me a plate of honeyed donuts for breakfast. I ate them with coffee and had just begun to write when there was a knock at the door. It was Guy, wearing dark glasses and an agitated expression.

"Aren't you supposed to have left for the mountains?" I asked.

"I couldn't leave without..." he began. "I've fallen a little in love, and..." he trailed off, sitting down.

"I'll make some coffee," I said, surprised and embarrassed, sensing there was more to come.

"My wife is very troubled. I can't understand her anymore," he continued, with tears in his eyes. "I want my marriage."

"Then you must tell her," I responded. This seemed to pacify him, so I went on a little about women and marriage until he thanked me and got up.

"Let's keep in touch," he said, giving me an affectionate hug and stepping out of my door, ready now for his mountain hike.

Love is not easy for women or men, I concluded, as I sat alone in my courtyard, enveloped in sunshine.

A BEACH ENCOUNTER

It was my first venture to the beach, a baking hot day in Agadir, in the early summer of 1989. Living among women who wore djellabas to cover every inch of their bodies in public had had its effect on me: I'd become modest, embarrassed even, at the thought of displaying my flesh for all to see; men, I mean. Until now, I'd tanned myself in private, in the courtyard of the house I lived in loaned to me by the mother of a Moroccan friend. But I longed to lie on the beach and swim in the ocean. The beach was a glorious stretch of pale soft sand, a mere five-minute walk from the house, and it was just too hot to resist anymore.

The tourists were over on their private hotel beaches, pink and topless on loungers, oblivious of all except the sun. The main beach was colonized by young Moroccans playing football and ogling any stray foreign women brave or foolish enough to lie at their feet, so I chose a spot a good hundred yards from them. I stretched out my towel, slid my skirt down my thighs as nonchalantly as possible, removed my T-shirt, and lay down quickly in my one-piece pink swimsuit, hoping I'd disappear into the sand.

The sky arched above me, blue as cornflowers, and dazzlingly clear. Everything was perfect: the lapping of the waves, the cries of the seagulls over by the fishing harbour, the echoes of the young men's voices; except I felt shameless and conspicuous, an invitation to all and sundry.

After a while, when a pool of sweat had formed beneath my back,

I sat up and looked all round: the coast was clear. I got up and walked slowly down the beach to the shore. Tiny clear frothy waves lapped and ebbed as I walked out, resolute, as if on a mission. I dove under and swam about in the gently rolling ocean, my only companions the shoals of silvery sardines that had so far escaped the fishermen's nets.

After a while, I walked swiftly back up the beach to my towel and lay down again, my body covered in droplets of sparkling seawater that turned quickly into patches of white salt. I breathed and closed my eyes; such bliss. And then I heard the light thump of footsteps on the sand getting closer. I turned over onto my stomach and turned my head in the direction the footsteps were coming from, my eyes hidden by my sunglasses. A young boy of about fourteen, barefoot and bare-chest, wearing ragged cut-off shorts, was approaching.

"Ey, madame want sex?" he called out, from a few feet away. I pretended to not hear him, to be asleep, and didn't move. "Madame, la gazelle," he said, repeating what all young Moroccan men said to every foreign woman, thinking that comparing them to a shy and frisky gazelle would do the trick. I ignored the comment, and he stepped closer, standing over me now, his dark shadow falling on me. At this, I lost my cool composure and peered up at him. "Safay," enough, I said. "Seer fehelek," go away, I added, repeating what a Moroccan friend had taught me.

That did it; to be rebuffed by a loose foreign woman speaking his language was too much in one day. "Huh," he snapped. "You could be my grandmother!" And off he strode.

THE DESERT SKY

Clouds of sand billowed up as the Land Rover wound its way across the flat bleak wasteland that leads to the Sahara. There were no signs, no piste, just faint criss-crossed tire tracks. It was early morning and the air was still quite fresh. Above and all around, from horizon to horizon, the sky enveloped us, a mad surreal blue, more cloudless blue sky than I'd ever seen. With my blue turban blowing like a flag in the dry desert wind, I sat gazing out of the open windows towards the horizon, where a backdrop of golden-amber dunes rose up like an apparition: granite peaks had been suddenly transformed into soft sand, the highest being the towering razor-edged Erg Chebbi.

I had made up my mind to see the desert and was travelling with a local driver and guide. After what seemed like hours of driving without getting any closer, we finally came to a last solitary outpost. A sparse settlement of concrete cubes, nothing green and a single well – how and why did people live in such a forsaken habitat? A few miles further on, we arrived at a roughly built hostel perched at the edge of the dunes. As the Land Rover came to a halt, a black-skinned man, whose ebony eyes seemed embedded in ivory, ran out to greet us. He took our bags and led us inside the hostel into a square courtyard, where I sat down on a bench and stared out through the open door at the sea of rippling sand. A lean young boy sat idly smoking on the doorstep. I felt becalmed, in an end-of-the-world silence. There was nowhere to go and nothing to do.

By mid-day, the sun had moved directly overhead and it was

scorching hot, so I moved inside to a cooler room with a stone floor. The wattle and bamboo ceiling was low, and frayed orange curtains flapped at glassless window frames in an occasional current of air. There was no electricity, and precious little water: none in the toilet, none in the taps. Soon, I heard the sound of chopping and of pots clanging, and before long the hostel keeper served us a simple lunch, a tajine, fatty and heavily spiced – impossible to tell if it was beef or even camel meat – which I ate more with gratitude and amazement than appetite.

As afternoon came around, I sat back without talking, reading or thinking while the heat quivered above the sand. I drifted in and out of sleep to the hypnotic creaking of door hinges, and to the sound of a hammer and a man's low voice chanting in time with it. And then the sounds stopped and there was only the drone of a solitary fly.

Around four o'clock, the calm was shattered. A blustery chergui wind picked up; doors banged open and shut, letting in flurries of sand. Outside, the desert had been transformed into a beige ocean of billowing, whirling waves with no distinction between sky and land. The distant huts of the settlement had vanished. The only thing I could see was a small herd of camels resting on their shanks, slowly chewing fodder, their huge protective eyelids disdainfully closed to the familiar occurrence. By now, my nose, ears and fingernails were filled with grains of sand, and my hair felt like gritty straw. The hostel keeper took pity on me and brought me a tumbler of water from a barrel to rinse my face and teeth.

Hours later, when the sandstorm had passed, the transition from royal blue twilight to pitch-black night happened swiftly. I lay on a hard divan, writing in the light of candles that cast lilting shadows on the rough, adobe walls. Then, I went outside where the wind had dropped and the temperature was falling fast. Towards the southeast, the huge silhouettes of the dunes rose up in the darkness and I began to walk towards them. My boots sank into the sand, and it became harder to climb the higher I went. When I reached the crest, about sixty feet up, I sat down on top of the world, wrapped in darkness. Apart from the moon, the only light anywhere to be seen in that immense landscape was a faint glimmer coming from the hostel. I felt myself weightless, reduced to air, in the midst of that infinite black velvet dome of twinkling stars. Land and sky were one, and I was a part of it. A meteor blazed across the sky, brightening the heavens for a few moments before burning out somewhere in the night. I closed my eyes and made a wish.

The guide's voice echoed suddenly in the stillness and I half-ran, half-slid back down the dunes. Over dinner, I tried to convey to him my magical experience, but the desert was his home so he merely listened and smiled. That night, we slept on mattresses spread out in the courtyard, covered by thick camel's wool blankets.

When I woke, there was just a hint of light low in the eastern sky. The guide was up, and together we went over to rouse the camel drover, who was asleep beside his animals. He rubbed his eyes and stood up quickly. The guide mounted a pale ivory-skinned beast. Meanwhile, I clung firmly to one the colour of sand as it unfolded itself from a kneeling position with a sudden lurch down and forwards. And then I rose to what seemed a great height. In the dawn half-light, with the drover walking in front, and with our two camels tethered together by a thin rope, we set off into the dunes. Seated on thick striped blankets, I soon fell into the rhythm of the animal's slow, sinuous and sturdy gait. As far as I could see, there was nothing except pristine sand and great rolling dunes – a terrain at once hostile and serene.

After a half-hour riding, the drover stopped. On the distant Algerian horizon, the first orange glow had appeared. And then, more quickly, the fiery sun emerged, couched between two crests, flushing the desert with golden light, and casting our shadows onto the dunes like black elongated cartoons. We dismounted and I stood on the night-cooled sand, watching the sun climb higher and higher in the sky. It was a dizzying realization that we were the only souls in this universe of sand. In the silence, emptiness and overwhelming peace, I felt small and close to the Creator of all things.

And then I had a strange sensation: an aching need to be somewhere familiar. I had come so far from home. We returned to the hostel for breakfast and when we drove away, with the dunes disappearing slowly behind us, I felt nostalgia. It was strangely liberating to be where there was nothing.

The Colonel & the Judge

The Colonel was there to meet me when I stepped off the train in Marrakesh onto a platform overrun by blood-red geraniums. I hadn't expected a man wearing a sports shirt and sunglasses. It was only when he was right in front of me, smiling broadly as though he already knew me, that I realized my mistake. We had been writing enthusiastic letters to each other for the past six months and were now finally meeting.

By the time my first three months in Morocco ended, I already had a plan – or a veiled excuse – to return. Instead of a novel, I would write a book about Morocco, about trees: seven of the trees that have been cultivated in Morocco's orchards and oases for thousands of years. The Colonel was a passionate botanist, had written a book about traditional herbal medicines and had responded to my romantic notion by appointing himself my mentor.

The Colonel was a short, solid man, a Berber from Azrou in the North. He had round brown eyes that twinkled with mischievous curiosity and humour, and a round olive-skinned face to match, topped by an army haircut that left only a veneer of spiky black hair on his scalp. I was completely in his thrall, especially because he'd somehow procured an apartment I could use until I found a place of my own. After stowing my bags in the trunk of his car, he drove away, entertaining me in guttural French with jokes, lines of poetry and Moroccan proverbs.

The pleasant light-filled apartment turned out to be in a putty-pink building in the rambling rose-filled gardens of the Hôpital Militaire, where the Colonel was Head of the Immunology Department. I stood on the wide balcony, breathing in air scented by rosemary hedges in the gardens below, and stared at the vista of snow-capped High Atlas Mountains, a formidable barrier, clear and close, that filled the entire sky south of the city.

"Wonderfully clear at this time of year, n'est-ce pas?" the Colonel said, puffing and then catching his breath. "Now, rest, everything you need is here. Tomorrow evening, I take you to a baptism in the Medina. We will start on your book in a day or so..." he finished, firmly in charge of the situation and of me.

By seven o'clock the next evening, I had gotten over my jetlag and spruced myself up a bit. With his wife Selwa, a delicate sloe-eyed woman with finely chiselled bones, seated beside him, the Colonel drove us through the great Bab Doukkala arch in the crenellated ramparts, into the Medina, where I had lived with Fatima. At night, the serpentine alleys are dark and deserted, fearfully mysterious to foreigners. In daylight, the same alleys bustle with life and a pageant of colourful people. We abandoned the car when the alleys became too narrow and continued on foot until we arrived at a deeply shadowed cul-de-sac. An imposing wooden door, set in a high sombre wall, stood ajar. Two young men in white djellabas waited beside it, greeting guests with lanterns.

When we stepped inside the huge mansion house, a scene of brilliant lights, gilt mirrors, gaiety and music instantly replaced the exterior shabbiness. The house was already full of distinguished-looking people. It seemed like a staged set, unreal, a dream in vivid colours. In the ornate cedar-carved reception salons, the men were assembled apart from the women, all of them clad in fine hand-sewn brown and white gandoras, white skullcaps and red fez hats, their white-stockinged feet tucked into traditional yellow leather open-backed slippers. The women, safe from public scrutiny, had taken off their hooded djellabas and scarves, and had gone to town with expensive finery. Manes of lustrous chestnut and black hair flew above a sea of extravagant satin caftans edged with gilt embroidery, pinched in at the waist with solid gold belts, and set off by gold bangles, rings and earrings. In the streets, no such exhibition is ever seen, to avoid tempting the evil eye, which really means not tempting the envy of others. Meanwhile, I envied the women's darkly exotic glamour and felt conspicuously ordinary, under-dressed and un-feminine. I only managed to console myself with the thought that I was the only woman there with blond hair and green eyes.

As I looked around, the Colonel came up close beside me. "That's the father, over there," he said. I looked across to a short, corpulent white-haired gentleman wearing immaculate white cotton robes and a fez hat, who was clearly the centre of attention. "He's eighty years old," the Colonel added. "This is the baptism of his seventeenth child!" There was an undeniable ring of masculine pride in his voice.

Suddenly I remembered something. "Is he a judge?" I asked.

"Yes, he is. Very well known in Marrakesh," the Colonel replied.

I was speechless. Just before leaving America, a young Moroccan woman had told me about her grandfather, a judge in his eightieth year with four wives, many children and countless grandchildren. She said I would find him fascinating and that I should meet him. She had even given me her mother's telephone number to make an appointment.

And now here I was in the house of the very same Judge! Westerners might call it a coincidence, but the Moroccans would say mektoub, it was written. I explained my astonishment to the Colonel, who seemed stunned, but then he walked over to the Judge to say something in his ear.

When the two men returned, the Judge immediately ushered us to some long divans in one of the salons. Before we had a chance to discuss the coincidence, the orchestra struck up to signal it was time for the baptismal celebration to officially begin.

"Will you dance with me, Madame?" said the Judge, looking down a prominent straight nose. The Colonel looked pleased, nodded at me and gestured for me to get up.

Although I couldn't imagine how or what we'd dance, I felt a dash of pride to have been asked by such an illustrious host, so I just smiled, "Oui, Monsieur, avec plaisir."

"But first, Madame, I must ask you…" the Judge paused. "Do you find me handsome?"

I sensed a potent hush all round us until, realizing there was no way out but innocent deception, I replied, "Oui, Monsieur. Vous êtes très beau." Everyone nearby began to laugh. The Judge laughed too, tickled to have won the game, and escorted me gallantly across the floor. I cannot remember what kind of steps or movements we made. I remember being taller than the Judge, feeling his arm grasp me firmly around my waist, his head held high and his sturdy belly close to mine as we turned around to the lilting Arab music in a roomful of dark watchful eyes.

After a few minutes, the Judge stopped dancing, perhaps a little tired or giddy, and took me to another divan over to the side in a sort of antechamber.

"So how do you like my country?" he asked. I enthused a great deal, though he seemed to be thinking of other things. "You know, I have four wives, seventeen children and forty grandchildren. And…" he paused, leaning a little closer as if to confide a secret. "I have many concubines of course."

I felt a moment's fascination, wondering what it would be like to be his concubine, and how I should reply to this disclosure. I decided to say nothing, to nod and smile rather vaguely instead. In a society where men and women are carefully kept at a distance, it was easy to see how a mere glance could be construed as enticement.

Our interview was cut short by the timely arrival of an attendant to advise the Judge that dinner was about to be served. I sat with the Colonel and Selwa, and with several other guests, at one of the large round brass tables that filled the salons. A troop of waiters in traditional costume brought ornate metal bowls over, which we held our hands in while they poured warm water over them, and then we dried them on linen towels. After this, the most sumptuous meal I have ever seen was set before us. The waiters brought us course after course, strutting theatrically all in a row, bearing silver trays above their heads with great ceremony. First came a bastilla, a filo-pastry pie the size of a bicycle wheel, filled with pigeon, eggs and almonds, and dusted with icing-sugar and cinnamon, which custom dictates be broken apart with the fingers. When we were done with the pie, having scattered pigeon bones all round the platter, the waiters deftly folded and removed the soiled white plastic tablecloth. Under it, I counted four more, one for each course. What an ingenious compromise: we could eat uninhibitedly, drip juices, but still have a clean cloth for the next course. A glistening half sheep mechoui that the Colonel informed me had been roasting in an earth oven for six hours, swiftly took the pie's place. I hesitated a moment to see the eating protocol. Dozens of well-trained fingers quickly ripped the piping hot meat apart and dipped the chunks into salt and cumin, before popping them with the greatest of ease into their mouths. I made much of chewing a few morsels as I had the feeling that all eyes were upon me, to see if I was impressed, if I was embarrassed to eat with my fingers or if I knew only to use the fingers of my right hand, even to gauge the size of my appetite.

When the sheep's carcass was cleared away, we were presented with a clutch of braised hens blanketed with green olives and preserved lemons, which, not surprisingly, everyone ate more slowly. I'd been hoping for some vegetables or something green, but meat is the status symbol of the rich and vegetables of the poor, and this gala definitely belonged to the former. The final dish, a colossal bowl of couscous, the steam rising from it thick with ginger and cinnamon, came with a heap of mutton hovering on top. This dish was clearly more for show than to satisfy hunger, although the couscous connoisseurs couldn't resist tasting a spoonful or two. Gilt-edged bowls of fruit arrived next, but were left untouched.

When the feast was over, we sank back against velvet-covered cushions and let the waiters pour more water, this time scented with orange blossom, over our well-oiled hands. Scalding mint tea was served next, which helped my digestion recover. At this point the Colonel rose, rubbed his stomach, grimaced and led us out into an immense colonnaded courtyard. Seated among the tall cypress and hibiscus bushes, some quite frenzied Berbers had taken over from the more sedate Arab musicians, who'd been serenading us with lutes during dinner. I was dying to ask the Colonel who the Judge's wives were and seized the moment. He glanced up towards the balcony windows where several bescarved women with babies and young children in their arms were staring down at the shenanigans that had taken over their household. There was no way of knowing if they resented or were relieved not to be taking part in it all. Such traditions do not change easily; the wealthier a man, the more he guards his womenfolk.

It is not customary for men and women to dance together, and most of them were as old as the Judge. Instead, the men watched the women dance, the rounded middle-aged and elderly ladies swaying their hips as sexily and expertly as the young ones. One or two of the younger men couldn't resist the music and stood to the side, clapping their hands exuberantly, rotating their hips just like the women, their arms stretched out high and wide. It was too much to resist, so I walked into the circle of women dancers, closed my eyes, let the rhythm seep into my body, and began twisting my hips. The women nearest me laughed, surprised to see me standing there, but they took my hands in theirs and we danced in twos and then in a ring, finally letting go of good manners.

When I remembered the Colonel, he was eyeing me with some surprise, pointing discreetly at his watch to signal it was time to leave. I was by then quite drunk from the richness of the occasion, although according to Islam's dictates, not a drop of alcohol had been served. As we stood at the door, the Judge came to wish us goodbye. He shook my hand and said to the Colonel, quite loudly, "Bring her again!"

An Evening with the General's Wife

I first met Rachida at an American friend's house. She was a petite woman of about thirty-five, lively and friendly. Her shining almond-shaped eyes were circled with dark shadows that gave her an air of weariness and melancholy. Over dinner, she told me about the American pianist, hired to play in the piano bar of the legendary La Mamounia, who had fallen madly in love with her, married her, and then promptly left her for another gig, never to return.

Not long after that first meeting, one late November evening, Rachida knocked at my door. "I'm going to visit Amina. She's the wife of a general. I think you'd enjoy meeting her. Would you like to come?" she asked, stepping through the arched doorway into my little house. I nodded and went quickly to change my clothes.

In the street, we hailed a 'petit taxi', ready for the inevitable car chase. At that hour, the brightly lit Avenue Mohammed V was choc-a-bloc with unruly traffic. Cars, mopeds, bicycles and horse-drawn carriages vied with each other and sped along in a haze of dust and gas fumes. Undeterred, our driver simply put his foot down and streaked brazenly in and out of anything that moved. We reached the junction with the road to Casablanca in one piece, and Rachida told the driver to stop at a secluded corner villa.

Despite the winter chill, bougainvillea blossoms tumbled thickly from the villa's imposing high walls. Hearing our voices, guard dogs barked ferociously into the night, but Rachida knew the house well and knocked sharply on the solid metal gate until heavy footsteps could be heard crunching on gravel. The gate opened and a soldier stood before us, half-hidden in the gloom. He wore khaki fatigues and a thick wool burnoose with the hood drawn deeply over his forehead; even so, I could see he was a young man with a stern, bony face and sunken dark eyes. He nodded at Rachida and eyed me with a frown, but when she explained who I was he stood back to allow us to enter. Once inside, we were in a damp shadowy garden, walking in tall grass among the dark silhouettes of the olive trees and ornamental palms that encircled the villa.

A door on a veranda opened and a woman appeared, smiling broadly, holding her arms out towards Rachida. They kissed on both cheeks several times, warmly and with a kind of urgency. The woman turned politely to me, shook my hand, kissed me and then we were inside the house, walking through the hallway.

Amina's husband had been with the late King Hassan II during the assassination attempts and the coups d'état. The General was currently in the Western Sahara while Amina was holding the home fort. I guessed her to be in her early fifties, well built, with a strong face and an authoritative matronly bearing that made her seem taller and larger than she actually was. The long robe she wore, a moss-green tkshita with embroidered slits, set off her titian hair that was twisted into a neat chignon at the nape of her neck. She wore no makeup, but gold rings and earrings added a touch of femininity to her otherwise austere appearance.

As we entered the room, I immediately noticed a small, slender woman dressed in red, reclining limply against the cushions on one of the plush velvet divans. Rachida seemed surprised to see her. Amina glanced at Rachida and then at the woman, sharing looks that expressed sadness, sympathy and rage all at once. I sat beside Rachida on a divan opposite the woman in red, while Amina sank into a stately armchair. The three women spoke excitedly and waved their arms and hands about in eloquent signals of distress. I stared at the woman in red, embarrassed but intrigued to be witnessing this intimate scene. Her long shiny black hair fell in tangles around her shoulders; her eyes were bloodshot and wet with tears that had left black kohl-stained traces down her cheeks.

I turned away and noticed the rifle leaning against the arm of Amina's chair. After a few minutes, the woman sat up a little as though revived by the company and Amina called out loudly. A servant girl appeared from a doorway at the far end of the room, and after Amina spoke briefly to her, she nodded and disappeared.

"Fatiha's husband beat her just now," Rachida began, frowning, still looking back and forth at the woman and at Amina. "He's done it before, but this time he said he was going to kill her. He's a powerful man, well known in Marrakesh. He gets crazy with jealousy." I supposed that explained the rifle.

"I'm sorry," Amina turned to me. "It's one of those things."

Before I could think of a response, the servant girl returned carrying a large tray with glasses, a sealed bottle of Johnny Walker Red, a bowl of ice cubes, two packs of Marlboro cigarettes and a tray of titbits. In Morocco, I was learning, there was one life in the streets and another behind the walls, invisible and unknowable unless you were invited inside.

While Amina poured large shots of whisky, Rachida opened a pack of cigarettes and handed them round. "Bsaha!" Amina toasted me, reaching down beside her armchair, on the opposite side to the rifle, to slide a tape into a small transistor radio. A powerful, but melancholy, male voice filled the room. The love song went on and on, in the Arab fashion, telling of the grief of unrequited love. At times, the voice soared to great heights of passion, at others it descended to the depths, to notes so low they vibrated in my body. I began humming under my breath, and my hand went involuntarily to my heart. Amina saw me and began shaking with laughter, reaching out her arms in a gesture that said, "You are one of us. Come in, come here."

Then Fatiha began to smile, and I smiled back. Rachida was holding her hand, while Amina poured us all more whisky. When the song finally ended, Amina slipped another tape into the deck. It was the unmistakable voice of the Arab diva Um Koulthoum, beloved of all Arabs, singing one of her famous songs of ill-fated love. Um Koulthoum had known since girlhood she must belong to all men, never just to one. As I listened, I wondered about this group of women I was now part of. Would Fatiha return to her jealous husband? Had Rachida got over the American who had come into her life and disappeared so soon? Did Amina miss her absent husband, and how did she bear the hours of solitude? And what was in store for me in Marrakesh?

The servant girl strode back into the room and placed a steaming beef tajine in the centre of the table. She kept her eyes averted and I couldn't help speculating about her life too, and what she thought of us. Amina handed round bread, and we all leaned forward to eat from the bowl with our fingers; even Fatiha ate a little.

From that moment, the evening began to take on a different tone. We drank more whisky, and smoked more cigarettes. Fatiha took a mirror from her purse and I watched, fascinated, as she began to apply lipstick, slowly but determinedly, all the time staring at her image in the mirror. Amina noticed too, changing the tape to a vibrant, more rhythmic, music and turning up the volume. Fatiha rose from the divan, shaking out her long black hair. Almost in a trance, she picked up her headscarf, tied it around her hips, knotting it thickly at the side, and then stepped into the centre of the room. Barefoot on the thick piled carpet, she began to move to the music's sensual rhythm, reaching her arms high in the air, twirling round and round, like a bird freeing itself from someone's grasp. Her hands and fingers wove seductively, and her hips gyrated deeply, as if she were reaching inside to her core.

It was captivating to watch her sad face come to life, to see her dark eyes flash and her scarlet lips and white teeth open in a triumphant smile. She was beautiful and sensual, and it was easy to see how her husband could be jealous. The room was suddenly filled with a shrill ululation. Amina and Rachida were spurring her on with a beating of the tongue – something I'd tried but knew I would never achieve. While Fatiha danced, we swayed and clapped to the music, and when I couldn't resist any longer I got up to dance beside her.

It was late when Amina roused the soldier, asleep in his hut, and instructed him to drive us home. The dark, damp night and the sudden silence of the yellow-lit, deserted streets cleared my head a little. I sat in the shadowy car, gazing at the soldier's dark form and at Rachida's dark face and eyes, and at her black hair that merged into the night, and no longer knew if I was blond or dark myself.

That evening, the door of isolation had closed behind me. I was in a new place, and there was no going back.

THE NIGHT OF THE FIFTIETH BIRTHDAY

It was May, the month I've always liked best, and the evening was clear and balmy, with a dusky sky like a bowl full of stars. My house in riad Zitoun Qdima – Old Olive Garden Street – was just a few minutes' walk from the Djemaa el Fna Square in the heart of the Medina.

The old house rose up tall amid the labyrinth, wall to wall with all the others huddled together behind the ramparts for safety, for warmth in winter, and for shade and coolness in the summer heat. With its two floors, courtyard and series of salons and terraces, the house was too large for me but the luxury of so much space proved both calming and inspiring. In a city so noisy and stimulating it can overload the senses; a quiet private place restores your equilibrium.

When I awoke that morning, I suddenly remembered it was my fiftieth birthday. At home, this would have occasioned a great fuss, but here, in the absence of family and friends, I had no plans to celebrate. I'd spent half the day doing chores; they took on a different quality here, and became instead simple pleasures. Washing the courtyard beneath the clear blue sky refreshed me; popping out to the bustling souk to buy food for lunch in alleys filled with spicy aromas sharpened my appetite, and hanging my washing on the rooftop gave me a sense of being a part of the community. The flat white roofs stretched out across the city, one leading to another, an alternative world to the enclosed and hectic life in the alleys below. The rooftops are the private domain of women; if any man appears on a nearby roof they immediately vanish, to prevent from catching a glimpse of the women without their all-concealing djellabas.

In the afternoon, while the rest of Marrakesh took its long daily siesta, I'd given myself up to sun worship, and would have been quite content to read after cooking myself dinner. But as the sun went down and left the courtyard in dark shadow, I felt the sting of solitude and recalled an invitation from Rachid, a local restaurant-owner, to drop by for a drink one evening.

In a summer dress and sandals, I stepped from my door into an alley just wide enough for men and mules to pass. Like the city's veins, the alleys course out in all directions from the Square until they reach the city's ramparts. Some are wide, some narrow; some are open to the sky; others are covered with rushes that shade them from the day's blistering heat. Full of wild characters and exotic wares, their effect on me was almost hallucinatory, bringing light-headedness, but sharpness too, a feeling of being near the edge of life where anything might happen. The contrasts of life go hand in hand: souks selling live chickens next to those offering elegant handicrafts; emaciated mules beside brand-new Mercedes, and ragged peasants alongside the well-suited gentry.

At that time of evening, the alleys are full of obstacles and surprises. Young men's eyes search out female prey. They have a piercing curiosity and a worldly look that is both attractive and unnerving. "Oh, la gazelle!" one called out, as I flushed with pleasure. I later heard every foreign woman being so compared, regardless of age or beauty. "Pour le plaisir des yeux," for the pleasure of the eyes; one of the bazaarists invited me inside his stall to inspect his goods. As I negotiated the noisy disorderly traffic, I jumped this way and that to avoid colliding with a scruffy mule heaving a wobbling cart and then a fearless moped driver on an urgent mission. Everything seemed about to crash into something or someone, but somehow missed by a hair's breadth without the batting of an eyelid. Pedestrians walked through it like sleepwalkers, amid the constant honking of horns, attuned to the slower rhythm that lay beneath the surface chaos. Once I had understood this, I learned to walk and cycle unperturbed.

As I came through a small arch, the great Berber market Square opened up before me. It was already in the throes of its nightly carnival, beneath a sky woven with mauve and pink silk flourishes. A warm reddish-apricot glow, like the lights of a film set, spread across all the ochre-washed walls, buildings and cafés that encircle the Square. It was this sensual colour that gave the city its name, Marrakch el Hamra, Marrakesh the Red. From all the alleys, crowds of people flowed into the Square, and in the centre a dense swarm surged in every direction, hungry for entertainment and refreshment. To reach the restaurant on the far side, I had no choice but to carve a path, elbowing my way past rapt audiences pressing in on storytellers; some of them were transvestite, and wiggled their skirted hips, pouting with crimson lips. I ducked to avoid a young acrobat flying through the air, and skirted the cobras stunned stiff by raucous flutes that reared up at my feet. At the heart of the revelry was the loud pulsing of drums and tin castanets, and the raw voices of the Gnaoua trance musicians.

From this pandemonium, I finally stepped through a regal doorway onto wide red-carpeted marble stairs, down into the vast tiled courtyard and pure calm of the El Baraka restaurant. Meaning good luck or blessings, the restaurant had once been the home of a pasha, the governor of a city. The courtyard was lushly planted with mulberry, banana palms, bougainvillea and night-scented jasmine. Candlelit tables sprinkled with rose petals were set here and there beneath the trees, and at each end of the courtyard was an opulently furnished dining salon hung with glowing Arabian Nights' lanterns.

Rachid was standing by the kitchen. He was a tall aristocratic-looking man dressed for his job in a brown double-breasted Western suit, a striking contrast to the blue cotton gandora he wore in the daytime. Almost the archetypical Arab, he had a portly frame and a dashing moustache. He caught sight of me and came quickly to greet me.

"It's my birthday," I said. "I thought I'd come and have a drink." Rachid kissed and congratulated me, leading me by the hand to a table beside a fountain, muttering something to a waiter clad in velvet waistcoat and impeccable calf-length pantaloons.

Guests began to arrive and Rachid went over to greet and seat them. I was sipping wine, looking up at the navy-blue night sky and enjoying the balmy evening air, when a man entered the courtyard, looking back and forth as if he'd walked in by accident. I saw Rachid go over to him; he gestured towards the courtyard and showed him to a table not far from mine. I glanced quickly in his direction, enough time to see he was not Moroccan.

The waiter brought the man a bottle of wine, poured a taster and then filled his glass. The man sat back, savouring the surroundings, and then looked at me.

"Are you alone?" he asked, leaning forward, speaking in French. I said I was. "May I join you?"

He said his nickname was Sammi, short for Samir; he was Turkish, on business in Marrakesh, and it was his first time in Morocco. He was a handsome man of about forty, slim, with bright light-brown smiling eyes. "All alone in Morocco?" he asked, shaking his head.

"Yes," I replied. I wasn't used to explaining what I was doing. Instead of asking me directly why I was alone, Moroccans would ask where my husband was. I would reply that he was away on business.

I ate dinner with Sammi and we drank another bottle of wine, talking about everything and nothing, laughing, both pleased to have chanced upon a companion. I told him it was my birthday, though not which one. "How brave to celebrate alone," he remarked.

When we left the restaurant, the nightly tumult was over in the Square. It was a different place now: dark and deserted, except for a body or two draped in a burnoose, spread out in a doorway. We walked arm in arm down the shadowy passages, where there wasn't a soul in sight and only an occasional dim street lamp to light our way. It was pitch-black inside the house. Sammi followed as I edged along the passageway to the kitchen, to light a lamp. He stopped, stepped nearer and took my face in his hands. I moved away and went to turn on the radio, hoping music would cover my emotions. But Sammi came towards me again and again. Each time, I let him kiss me, but then another part of me pushed him away. He smiled. "Listen. What we do will hurt no one, and may feel very good…"

I let Sammi undress me in the shadows of the courtyard. My clothes were scattered here and there on the tiles when he knelt in front of me. What he did then felt like a sweet homage. Soon, he drew me into the bedroom and lit the lamp; Sammi wanted so much to make love to me, he made me want to too. I looked at him lying in the pink light, he was a stranger but someone I did not feel strange with. He was right; I was far from home, on a solitary pilgrimage. We had met and moved towards each other out of time, out of place, in a city that celebrated every moment.

Sammi knew the art of pleasure well. We rested close to each other and didn't speak any more, and the hours passed unnoticed until he woke me around dawn.

"I have to go, but I don't know where I am," he said, looking at me in amazement. "I haven't done anything like this in years!" We both laughed and got dressed. I walked with him into the empty alley, pointed to the left and told him to keep walking until he came through the arch into the Square. There was always a 'petit taxi' or two circling around, whatever the hour.

I watched Sammi walk away and when I closed the door, I could feel tears in my eyes. Standing in a blaze of soft morning sunshine, I remembered I was fifty and a day now. I thought how beautiful and how harsh life was, but it was good that way.

A Fateful Meeting

I met him on a bus on my way back to Marrakesh after a trip to
Tiznit, a Berber stronghold in the deep south of Morocco. I was
writing when he stepped on board, but I glanced up quickly to look
at him, in the way one does, a sort of reflex action to inspect one's
travelling companions. He was ruggedly handsome, of medium
height and bore himself like a man of thirty or so, or perhaps it was
his strong, solid build that gave me that impression. Most young men
had slender, more effeminate bodies and the finely chiselled bones of
the Berber race. His smooth skin caught my eye, the colour of café
crème, and his tightly curled black hair was trimmed neatly, close
to the scalp. His lips were full, the African in him, but he had the
straight proud Arab nose. There was about him an aura of kindness,
pride, intelligence and warmth. You can see and feel a lot about a
person in one brief moment, I thought, looking away when his eyes
met mine, as if censuring myself. Even so, I had the distinct feeling
that through my eyes, I had touched him. He had that undeniable
physical presence that sends out waves of feeling. I returned to my
writing, blithely unaware of what had happened to me.

But then he was speaking to me, politely, showing me a ticket:
"You are in my seat, Madame." Noticing the bags at my feet and in
the rack above me, he signalled quickly that I should stay put. He
took the empty seat behind me and I smiled and thanked him.

The bus followed the old caravan route from Timbuktu, crawling
first through the arid Anti Atlas Mountains, and then through the

far-flung ranges of the High Atlas. I closed my notebook to watch the landscape. It was spring, April, and I was relieved to see the countryside lush and green again, reviving from the long drought with the help of the recent March rains. I almost felt physical pain when the earth became parched and turned to rutted dust. Now, the countrywomen were out in the fields weeding their crops, dressed in skirts and scarves of bright reds, orange and pink. Some were standing at stone wells filling jars, balancing them on their head as they walked off towards a distant settlement. Scarlet poppies and yellow calendulas swayed amid silver grasses and short rye. The almond blossom had already fallen, and the slender black trees were in full leaf on the mountain terraces. The melodic voices of the other passengers accompanied my reveries until, about half way on our five-hour journey, the bus came to a stop at a small café.

We were on a stony windblown plain in the middle of nowhere. On one side of the road hills of red clay spread across the distant skyline, on the other, grey sandstone ridges filled the horizon. In between, there was nothing but open space in all directions, and a vast blue sky that came down to meet it everywhere I looked. The smells of dust, earth and grasses hung lightly in the breeze, and monotone Berber music blared from the café's radio. I sat close to the bus to keep an eye on my belongings, at a table beneath a tattered awning and sipped sickly-sweet mint tea. Moroccans love this intense sweetness, an all-purpose salvo: a reminder of the sweetness of love, a good luck charm against the bitterness of life and something to do to while away the hours.

The bus horn echoed in the still dry air and we returned to our seats. The man asked me what time it was. He seemed less confident now, younger than I had first thought, and I started talking to him, looking back through the opening between the seats. We spoke as usual in a combination of French, Arabic and English – each trying to speak at least a little of the other's language – but we were soon at a loss, and settled on French.

I described my travels and adventures in his country, and he eyed me with shining dark-brown eyes. How could I, he asked, a foreign woman alone, have done all this?

"W'Allah, you know my country better than me!" He spoke of his family with loyalty and love. His mother was from the Tafilalet region close to the Sahara, his father from Fès, which accounted for his mixed features.

When the bus finally flew past the silver-leafed olive groves on the outskirts of Marrakesh, he asked for my notebook and wrote a telephone number in it, making me promise to call. "I would like you to come to dinner with my parents," he said. "They will like to meet a foreigner like you."

At the terminus, I stepped from the bus into the burning dry heat of Marrakesh and into a clamouring horde of porters and would-be guides. I was used to them and said, "Seer fahalek," go away. But he stepped in front of me and took hold of the heaviest bags.

"Where are you going?" he asked. I told him I had rented a house in the Medina, not far away, and the friend who had found it for me would pick me up. "Will you be alright?" he replied, as we stood on the sidewalk on the noisy swarming street.

I heard the concern in his voice and told him not to worry. And so, he hailed a taxi and I waved as it sped away. I didn't know until much later, when our affair began, that halfway home he had asked the taxi driver to turn around and had gone back to the bus station to see if I was still waiting.

THE NIGHT I THOUGHT I WOULD DIE BEFORE MORNING

I first met A. when he came to the Moroccan restaurant where I had found work as dinner host. He was plump and talkative, as queer as they come, but quite entertaining. His reddish face dripped constantly with perspiration, with all the joking and gesticulating he was prone to, which caused his spectacles to be forever sliding down his nose. That evening, he was accompanied by his young friend, Jamal, who was a strikingly beautiful dark-skinned youth. A. was so taken with life in Marrakesh, that he had bought an old house in the Medina, not far from the restaurant.

A few days later, I was invited to the house-warming. It was quite a fiery event, held in the courtyard, and lit by the moon and a host of blazing candles. Gnaoua musicians exorcised the guests of their demons with their hypnotizing chants and raucous castanets, and the banquet of foods and fruits sated their appetites. I sat over by the musicians, who I knew because they also played at the restaurant. A few Moroccan youths stood idly staring and wondering, but the majority of the guests were A.'s French and Italian friends, dressed in the latest fashion, that had flown over to see his exotic lover and house.

Typical of those in the Medina, the house stood in a blind alley, in an impenetrable maze designed to confound invaders. You had to pay careful attention going there so you'd know how to get out and how to return another day. The house was spacious, with the usual three elaborately painted high-ceilinged salons opening into the courtyard; an upper floor with three more salons that gave onto a balcony, and a rooftop terrace with a panoramic view of roofs, sandstone minarets, palm trees and shimmering Atlas peaks.

Since A.'s house was near the restaurant, and he would only be coming to Marrakesh as often as his work – the nature of which I never quite understood – permitted, I asked him if he would rent me a room. A. agreed; the rent would be one thousand dirhams a month – more than half my wages at the restaurant. A young man called Mohammed would keep an eye on the house and pay the bills, and a woman called Zoubida would be housekeeper.

I chose a ground-floor oblong salon with high ceilings of carved and painted cedar, and double doors that closed with an iron bolt. Shiny mosaic tiles in blue and green climbed half way up the walls, and two low windows opened onto the courtyard. At one end of the room stood a four-poster double bed and at the other end I placed a small round table, a sturdy chair of woven rushes, and a makeshift metal clothes rack that I draped with a swathe of yellow cloth.

Mornings in the house were my favourite times. I would awake, just before dawn, to the insistent chants of the muezzin; perched high in the sky in their slender square minarets, they called the faithful to prayer, a chorus of male voices that rang out hauntingly in the clear morning sky. After them, the neighbour's cockerel would take up the challenge and crow at full tilt, followed by the sparrows arguing in the lemon trees and the garbled calls of street vendors. Finally, I would rouse myself as the rays of sunshine streamed in through the windows that I always left half-open. I rose each day to find Zoubida setting breakfast on the courtyard table, or hanging my washing on the rooftop, and felt a warm wave of pleasure and satisfaction. This was how you should live in Marrakesh.

But when A. arrived on his sporadic stays, it saddened me to see everything change. He fussed over the household details, and took to ordering Zoubida about as if he were a pasha. He had many guests, in addition to Jamal; young Moroccans whom he seemed to view as sexual trophies. I spent most of my time avoiding them, either up on the roof or in my room. He and Jamal went out every evening and would come back very late, noisily crashing through the heavy front door. At other times, there were hushed meetings with strangers. I suspected drugs and was soon proved right when Jamal unveiled a brick of marijuana about a foot wide hidden behind a curtain in the bathroom.

Things got worse. A. lectured me about the Moroccan man I was seeing, forbidding him to stay overnight in the house because it would upset the neighbours. He supported his case by saying they would do their gris-gris magic on me to make me leave. I was angry and speechless to hear this from a man who flaunted his own illicit relationships. My peace was gone.

A few days after this discussion, A. left for Paris again. Alone in the house a few nights later, I lay in bed thinking about what he'd said, drifting slowly to sleep. Suddenly, I was startled by a loud crash. I leaped out of bed, my heart throbbing in my ears, and crept into the pitch-black courtyard. I looked around, waiting for a movement, for a shadow, for someone to jump out at me. Hearing and seeing nothing, I tiptoed from one salon to the other until I came upon the shards of a large vase spread across the stone floor. I stared at the mess, wondering how it had happened.

After peering nervously behind the doors in all the rooms, upstairs and down, I went back to bed and told myself it must have been one of the neighbourhood cats looking for scraps. But my imagination got the better of me. All I could think of were the evil spirits the Moroccans call djnoun that they believe possess people and cause all the evil and sad things that happen to them, and that only exorcism can rid them of. I was used to being alone, but now I was terrified. There was no telephone in the house to call for help, and the neighbours now seemed like enemies. I was trembling, convinced I was being threatened by a djin, and suddenly the thought was in my head that I was going to die. I had no idea how or why, but I was going to die before the morning.

If I got dressed and left the house, it was already midnight, where would I go? I had no choice but to go through this alone. I remembered hearing there were good and bad djnoun, and that the bad ones fled at the sight of the Koran, so I placed the copy I had recently purchased beside me on the pillow. I remembered too how Moroccans fight the djnoun, dousing doors and drains with milk to prevent them entering through the cracks at night when we mortals are asleep and most vulnerable. I went to the kitchen and took the milk jug with me to the front door and to the courtyard drains, splashing the white liquid all around them. All I had to do now was sit the night out, so I held the Koran against me and prayed to God to save me – wondering whether I should call on Allah instead.

I sat upright in that anxious state for what seemed like hours, keeping my vigil until something stirred me from the half-sleep I'd fallen into. I strained my ears; it was not the muezzin's sombre dawn call from the mosque down the alley. Then I heard it more clearly, with my eyes open wide. It was the sound of singing, otherworldly and angelic, coming from somewhere in the hushed night. The muezzin don't sing, they chant in monotones; these voices were singing notes so high and pure that I could only conclude I was hearing a heavenly choir. I admit I felt a moment of rapture as I listened without moving or breathing, hoping it wouldn't stop, feeling like the only human awake and alive in God's otherwise silent universe.

Sometime later, still semi-conscious, I recognized with certainty the familiar sound of the muezzin, and then fell soundly asleep, no longer feeling alone.

The next thing I knew, warm shafts of sunlight were bathing my arms and face. And then I heard the street sounds: it was a day like any other. I hadn't heard Zoubida come in; she was singing and clunking crockery in the kitchen. I was alive; I hadn't been claimed by the djnoun!

That morning, I made up my mind to move. On my way to Gueliz, I took an unfamiliar passage and entered a small sandy square in the middle of which stood a very old, gnarled olive tree. In the centre of the square was a garden overgrown by weeds; around it stood a terrace of small high-walled houses, nine in all. The house nearest the olive tree had an arched wooden door painted electric blue, the colour used to ward off the evil eye. Without seeing inside, I wanted it to be, and somehow knew it would be, my next home.

An Unforgettable
Cup of Coffee

I awoke later than usual. The house was silent, the sun's brilliant rays creeping warmly across the courtyard. Zoubida usually roused me early with her clatter when she did yesterday's dishes and prepared breakfast. She would squeeze orange juice, make coffee with steamed milk, and slice a freshly baked baguette that she served with bowls of pale country butter and apricot confiture.

But Zoubida hadn't come. I had no idea why not. Perhaps she was sick, or just didn't feel like coming today. I would make breakfast myself. I pulled on a pair of Arab pantaloons, put on my flip-flops, grabbed a few dirhams from the bowl on my table and pulled the heavy front door closed behind me. Suddenly, life in all its aspects assailed me: voices echoed through the alleys, children's and street vendors'; a mule brayed loudly and agonizingly, as if in complaint at the load he was bearing. Down the alley, a miscellany of smells flowed one into the other - animal dung and rotting garbage from the pails left out vied with the appetizing odours of warm bread, olive oil and cumin that wafted from the open doors. And the smell of water and dust hung over everything, as housewives rinsed their homes and sluiced the water out into the alley, dampening the dirt.

The house I was living in was off derb Halfaoui, in a narrow passage that led into the bowels of the medina. Featureless and unwelcoming, the stark walls rose up on either side fifty or so feet, dilapidated, washed dark cinnamon. There was nothing soft, nothing green and nothing beautiful, except perhaps the doors to the houses. Low and thick and rough, they guarded the entrances, bearing heavy iron knockers and huge studs and keyholes.

I'd only gone a few steps in the passage when I met one of my neighbours, Samira, walking towards her house, a black plastic bag in one hand, a baguette sticking out the top. You had to stop to speak to anyone you knew, even if you'd only met them once. You had to acknowledge them, look into their eyes, and touch them - if not with a kiss on each cheek, at least with a handshake. You had to ask how they were, and how was their family? "Sabah el khir," good morning, I said. "La bes, qul shay la bes," Samira replied with a warm smile. Samira was widowed and lived alone with her young son; this much I knew. How she got by, I had no idea.

"Where are you going?" Samira asked. I told her Zoubida hadn't come, I was going to buy bread. "Aji, come have coffee with me," she insisted, laying her hand on my arm and drawing me towards a door on the opposite side of the passage to mine. I hadn't washed and my hair was uncombed. Unlike the women of the medina, I never wore a scarf, a useful way to hide unkempt hair.

I followed Samira down a stone step and through the low doorway. Entering these bleak-fronted homes always led to a moment of discovery. You might find a palace sparkling with mosaics and tiles, with columns, and a garden of cypress and bougainvillea. These were the riads of rich merchants. Without such a garden, you found yourself in a dar, a house with a simple open courtyard. The house I lived in, in which I had rented a room from a Frenchman who rarely came to visit, was a dar, but had been well kept and restored.

Samira's house was a sad affair; either the interior had never been completed, or it had simply fallen into ruinous disrepair. At one end of the courtyard, next to a crumbling wall, was a salon, its high wooden doors wide open. At the other end there was a crude kitchen without doors, open to the elements. I sat down on a low stool at a round table in a corner of the half-tiled courtyard, while Samira put water on to boil. She kept talking, while she prepared the coffee and cut up the bread. Did I like living in Marrakesh? Yes, I loved it, I said. Where was my husband? I was divorced and my husband had since died, I said. Did I have children? Yes, I had two sons.

As I answered, I was thinking about her life, and comparing it with mine. We were both alone, but while I had choices, she clearly did not. I was educated, while she was not. I felt uncomfortable with pity, but could find no other suitable emotion. And then I thought how I was living on the edge too, earned little money, gave no thought to pensions and the future; others might pity me.

Just then, the coffee started to percolate. I heard it bubbling loudly and as it did, its delicious aroma drifted across to me. Samira arranged a tin tray with two glasses, the coffee pot, a jug of frothy milk, a plate of bread, and two saucers, of butter and jam, just like Zoubida did, and brought it to the table and sat down.

The coffee was lightly spiced with cinnamon and cardamom, and was the best I'd ever tasted. I sat sipping it, savouring every mouthful, almost ashamed at my amazement that such a delicious thing could have been made in such abject surroundings.

I have never forgotten that morning, the cup of coffee, Samira's hospitality, and the dignity she maintained, even in poverty.

Zohra's Ladder

I had chosen the little house in Arsat el Hamid from the feeling I got looking at it from the outside. When the owner showed me inside, its charm bore out my sixth sense. It was welcoming and familiar, yet full of the promise of discovery, like meeting someone you had noticed from a distance and whom you liked instantly.

Once inside the thick high walls, I was in a very private little fortress of my own. At its centre was a pretty yellow and white-tiled courtyard with two lemon and three bitter orange trees. Everything was light and bright: dazzling whitewashed walls, blue doors and window shutters that were like patches of radiant sky. The shade the trees gave during the sun's journey across the heavens shifted indolently from one part of the courtyard to another, and I would move my chair accordingly.

The rooms were set around the courtyard; my bedroom looked out on the trees, and a delicate jasmine slinked and blossomed through the window grille, leaving its sweet sensual scent hanging in the air. Next to the bedroom was a small room in which I left only a rush mat for yoga. In the second tiny bedroom I placed a mattress for a guest. Next, set back from the courtyard, was the pomegranate-pink shower room for which I had invested in a primitive gas water heater that had to be lit with a match. It terrified me for it always seemed on the point of exploding.

The kitchen, if it can be called that, lay behind a sweeping arch in one corner of the courtyard. It consisted of a deep sink, a dish drainer and a solid concrete counter on which I kept my meagre supply of kitchenware and a crude three-ring gas cooker. There is no piped gas in Marrakesh, so like every other household I had a big gas cylinder, and when it ran out, sometimes in the middle of cooking, I would run to the local hanout and have another one wheeled to my house. Open to all the elements – sunshine, fresh air and breezes as well as white-hot sun, wind, sandstorms, rain and winter chills – my open-air house was a pleasure-dome in summer, but an igloo in winter. Crawling from my warm bed on a freezing December morning to make coffee in the open kitchen, or stumbling across the courtyard to the toilet in the dead of night, was a truly painful penance.

I filled the house with ceramic bowls and vases of garden roses bought from the souk at one dollar a dozen, and wrote for hours in undisturbed peace. In summer, I basked in the sun on my rooftop, beneath flapping sun-bleached laundry. In the evenings, I sat under the stars beside the lemon trees, and when winter came around, I lay under thick blankets on my mattress, listening to music and the night sounds of the square.

Meriam, one of the cooks at the restaurant, cleaned my house once a week. Black-skinned, with a round shining face, she was constantly smiling. Her voluptuous body was always hidden beneath a candy-pink djellaba, and I would hurry to receive the hugs she gave me, in which I melted like a child into the soft shelf of her bosom. Meriam was efficient and thorough, and such fascinating company that it was well worth the fifty dirhams I paid her. She would cook lunch the day she came, but was not used to eating with her employer and was too shy to sit down and share it with me.

One autumn evening, I got dressed up to go to dinner with Dana, an American friend. The nights had turned cool so I pulled my black burnoose around my shoulders. The entrance to my house consisted of a sturdy wooden door, with another smaller arched one set within its frame. The big door was only opened when Meriam washed the floors and swished the water outside. For everyday coming and going, I used the small door, stepping over the ledge and ducking, like walking through a hoop. Both doors were secured by one large lock that was old and rusted, and needed quite a bit of encouragement, some twisting and joggling, before it would open. That evening, after turning the knob several times, wondering if I'd be lucky enough to find a 'petit taxi' without waiting too long, I realized the door wasn't opening. I began pulling, tugging, shaking, and then finally kicked the door, but it still refused to budge. Eventually, I was forced to admit I was firmly locked inside my house. I looked at the high walls I loved for the privacy they gave me. Now they had become a prison. There was no way to climb them, nor any window to shout from, so I paced up and down the courtyard. And then I remembered the ladder I used to take my laundry up on the roof. From there, I could look down into my neighbour Zohra's house and call for help. Of all the neighbours, she was the one who always wished me a kind 'bonjour.'

I leaned the ten-foot ladder against the wall, gathering the voluminous burnoose around me, climbed to the top and walked to the edge of my roof where it met Zohra's.

"Zohra!" I called out, peering down into her home – something neighbours never do in Marrakesh. I could hear loud music and guessed her eldest son was home. "Zo-hra!" I yelled again. Zohra came rushing into the courtyard, looking this way and that. I yelled another shrill, "Zohra!" She looked up and saw me, a black form hanging over her roof.

"Skun? Skun?" who is it, she called out in a high-pitched panicky voice.

"It's me," I shouted, trying to sound calm.

"Ah, Pa-méla. Qu'est-ce que c'est?" What is it? Zohra asked.

I explained that my door wouldn't open, but she just frowned. I threw down my keys and at last she seemed to understand. She came around outside my door, and from my perch on the roof I could just see her tinkering with the lock. "La, la, maquadamsh," it's not working, she called out, shaking her head and returning to her house. Then, below me, Zohra appeared with her own ladder and set it against the wall right beneath me, pointing and beckoning.

"You go out this way," she explained, finding the obvious solution.

I climbed down into her house – it was the first time I'd been inside – and we both began to laugh at the absurdity of it all. "But what about when I come home?" I asked.

"Knock at my door, you come back in," she replied, without a second thought. I said it might be late and wouldn't want to disturb her.

"No problemo," she said, waving her forefinger in a way that meant I mustn't worry.

I found a taxi and arrived at Dana's house. We ate dinner, drank some good red wine and I told her the tale. We were used to such stories; life in Marrakesh had a way of tripping foreigners up. When I knocked at Zohra's door again, it was near eleven o'clock. The square was still and full of shadows. The cats were moaning their strange night laments beneath a misty moon as I scaled Zohra's ladder and then climbed down my own, into my house.

As I lay on the mattress on the floor, I began to laugh out loud. I'd have to do the same thing all over again the following morning to fetch the locksmith. I was lucky to have a neighbour like Zohra.

The Street Cleaner's Clothes

Street life in the Medina is a daily theatre, with shows from morning until night. Something about the light – sometimes the suffused glow of the sun, sometimes the harsh light of bare bulbs – the vivid and gaudy colours, people's uninhibited movements and exuberant voices, make the streets seem like movie sets.

In my house in Arsat el Hamid, I lived the two aspects of Arab life, the private and the public. Inside, everything is hidden, peaceful and protected; outside, everything is visible, drama and commerce. The magic threshold between the two is the front door, often imposing and ornate, compared with the deceptively derelict plain walls. Once outside my door, the world began and I was just another actor in a cast of thousands.

The neighbours accepted my presence tacitly, except for a curious stare now and then, and got on with their business. In the wide, open square lean cats lazed in the sun or in the shade if it was too hot. The local children played exuberantly in the dirt, at home-made spinning tops and toy cars made out of tin cans. Young men held hands in doorways, smoking, out of sight of their strict elders, joking, and clapping as they sang their favourite songs. Old men scuffed along in the sand in their slippers, their bony hands grasping their worry beads and walking sticks. Mornings would begin with the women washing their courtyards and swilling the water out through their front doors into the square. During the day, they came and went to the souk in rhythm with the firmly set meal times – snacks and fast food have no place in the Moroccan diet – and the square would fill with rich, irresistible aromas. Now and again, a car would drive through, or a bicycle or motorcycle, but for the most part, we were left alone, in peace.

The morning after I moved in I woke early, around six o'clock, with the clarion call of the neighbour's cockerel. It was easy to get up; the house was so quiet and pretty, full of light warm sunshine. I'd have my first coffee in my new home. After searching high and low, I couldn't find a match to light the gas, so I stepped out into the square, just as I was, tousle-haired, and wearing slippers, hoping the hanout keeper on the corner had opened his doors for trade. The shutters were still down, and I was about to go back indoors and dress to cycle to the souk when I noticed an old man with a gaunt and furrowed face and straggles of silver-grey hair curling around a ragged turban. He was slowly sweeping the square with a long palm frond, gathering the litter into a small handcart. He looked up and waved a kind of salute.

"Sabah el khir." He wished me good morning, putting down his palm frond and shuffling up to me.

"Sabah el khir," I replied, shaking the bony hand he thrust towards me.

It occurred to me he might have a match. When I asked, he made no reply but began to reach beneath his tattered gandora into the folds of an undergarment. It took him a while to find the right pocket; each time he tried, he shook his head, pulled out his hand, and burrowed deeper into another layer of clothing. Again he rummaged, lifting the endless layers, slowly and deliberately, shaking his head again and taking out his hand, still empty. I almost laughed out loud, for it appeared that the old man was wearing his entire wardrobe. Instead, I began to wonder what other items were stored within their depths, and how or when he washed them all.

It seemed rude to rush him, he was putting so much effort into the search and seemed so sure he had matches somewhere if only he could unearth them, so I waited patiently. He began to search in the pockets on the other side, and at long last, his hand came out grasping a crumpled yellow matchbox.

"Mezziene," I said, applauding. I told him I'd light the gas and bring the matches back. He merely nodded, making a gesture as if he was smoking, and I understood he wanted a cigarette for his trouble. He seemed happy with the three I gave him and went back to his slow sweeping, while I made myself the coffee that had begun the whole rigmarole. In all that time, the old man had barely uttered a word.

I saw the old street cleaner almost every morning after that. Often, he would be taking a break from his sweeping, sitting on the ground propped against a wall with a tray of breakfast things in front of him. It was always in the same spot, but the tray was different, with a different teapot and glass.

One morning, I understood why when I saw Zohra bring him out a tray with bread and tea. All the neighbours took turns to give the old man breakfast. I took my turn from that day on, adding a cigarette or two that I watched him savour before continuing his work.

OBSERVING PROCESSIONS

It was a blistering afternoon. The August temperature had been soaring day by day, and the heat had so invaded my body that I felt one with it. I was reading in the shade of the lemon trees, when an uncanny low chanting sound wafted through the drowsy silence in the square. It seemed far away, so I didn't stir. A few minutes later, the chanting grew louder and closer, so I went to the door to see what it was. A hundred or more men, wearing all manner of clothes – suits, overalls, gandoras and jeans – were marching slowly and solemnly, with their heads bent down, chanting in unison behind a bier that was held on high by four men at the front of the procession. It was a humble wooden plank set on two long poles on which the dead body lay, wrapped tightly in a cream linen shroud, the outline and even the limbs and features of the body quite evident.

There wasn't a woman to be seen as the procession advanced. Any soul, or car, or mule, or bicycle, that came upon the procession either stopped, stepped aside, or joined it at the rear, so that no one would be in front of it and the way ahead was open. The chanting was a prayer, a psalm that ushered the soul to heaven, and was intoned with such a low fervent intensity that I shivered, standing there unseen as the procession passed by me.

There were constant processions, apart from funerals. There were even processions when a boy was circumcised. Dressed in white shirt, green velvet trousers and vest embroidered with gilt thread, the little tot, usually no more than three or four years' old, would be set in front of his father, astride an Arab stallion, with ornamented saddle and reins. Muskets were fired after the circumcision – carried out by the local barber whose unenviable job it has been for centuries – along with the women's ululations. I often heard the shots resounding through the square and nearby streets. All this drama compensated and distracted the boy from the pain and fear. He was riding on high, surrounded by men of all ages. He was going to be like them not like the women. After the ritual, I would see the boys dressed in little white shirts that reached their ankles, walking awkwardly with their legs wide apart as their wounds began to heal.

Wedding processions were led by a mule and cart that bore gifts to the bride-to-be's house; sacks of sugar and flour for daily life, and mirrors, clothes, perfume for beautifying. A gold belt was given to the bride at the marriage ceremony itself. Following the cart would be the extended family, the neighbours, and any passers-by that felt like joining in. There would be a dozen or so musicians, with hand drums and shrill flute-like instruments, all loudly singing and clapping and swaying to the beat as the procession lurched forwards on its way from one quartier to another. At dawn, after the night-long marriage ceremony, those with cars formed a cavalcade that would wind its ways through the streets, jubilantly honking their horns as they accompanied the bride and groom to their home.

After a while, it dawned on me that the processions augured a week of celebrations in the families' homes. Some were a pleasure to hear, with joyful music echoing through the alleys and in through my windows, but if the revellers had discovered amps and microphones they became unbearable. Often I would lie, unable to sleep, until the early hours of the morning, my ears stretched to their limits. Once, at the end of my rope, I went off in search of the house where the revelry was taking place. If you can't beat them, join them. When I located it, and was peering through an arch in a side alley, a group of women dragged me in and I found myself caught up in a dense throng, seeing only dark laughing eyes, the gleaming teeth of a hundred smiles and gold and red satin everywhere. A procession or celebration is surely about losing yourself in a community, becoming part of something larger than the self for a moment. It was always due to my neighbours' insistence that I came to know and feel all this.

Mr. Idrissi's Advances

In the house next door, on the other side of Zohra's, there was a couple with a drove of children. One day, I passed the mother on the way back from the souk, and when I saw her face I was surprised to see she was European. In the street, she always wore a djellaba and the compulsory scarf to cover her hair. Even her face had taken on the olive-brown skin tone of a Moroccan, and the staunch expression of a strict Muslim wife, so I hadn't, until then, recognized one of my tribe.

After lunch one day – two quiet hours when one's filled one's belly, took a siesta, and avoided the sun's burning climax – there came a knock at my door. I was surprised to see the European woman's husband standing there. He was small and dapper, with neatly cut grey hair, and wore a black close fitting chalk-stripe suit.

"I heard the mad boy with his truck last night and wondered if you were frightened," he asked, edging forward as though wanting to be invited in. "Abdellah Idrissi," he introduced himself. "I work with the police administration…" he said, leaving the word hanging and edging even further towards me. I hesitated, and then, thinking it would be a good idea to be neighbourly, I opened the door wider so he could step inside.

The mad boy he spoke of, lived in the terrace on the other side of the weed garden. He had caused quite a ruckus in the night. He'd parked his truck outside my door, and I'd heard the shrieks of laughter of his female company. In the early hours, a beer bottle had come crashing into my courtyard; his way, I assumed, of showing displeasure at a foreigner living in his square.

"If he gets crazy like that again, as you have no phone I was thinking you could knock on your wall with a rock," he said, seeming gratified to be inside my house.

"That's very kind," I replied, not quite understanding what that would do for me. Was he intending to rush out and kill the mad boy on my behalf?

Mr. Idrissi sat down at the wicker table in the courtyard and lit a strong-smelling cigarette. "I've seen a man coming in here," he went on in a tight voice, looking at me for my reaction. I merely smiled and gave a slight nod. "You know that's illegal here. We don't permit Moroccans to have relations outside marriage, and it's the same law for foreigners," he finished what he'd come to say, and pulled on his cigarette.

"He's a friend. He's teaching me Arabic," I replied, shrugging.

"Well, of course, if you'd come with me for a drink tonight," he said, leaving the rest of his sentence unsaid. I tried quickly to think of something to say that wouldn't seem like a rejection, and wouldn't incur Mr. Idrissi's ensuing wrath.

"You're a good-looking woman, why aren't you married?" his curiosity was getting the better of him, and I didn't want it to get the better of me. As he took my hand in his, I grinned and played for time. A flat "no" would be like a red rag to a bull, so that was out. A "yes" would no doubt later get me into a worse situation than I was already in.

"Well, I'm working tonight. Perhaps we can find another evening soon," I heard myself say sweetly. Mr. Idrissi must have been happy with that because he stubbed out his cigarette, got up and walked to the door.

"Got to get to work," he said, with a small glint of satisfaction in his hooded brown eyes. "Until we meet again, then, Madame!"

In the days that followed I heard nothing more from Mr. Idrissi, nor did I see his wife, for which I was very thankful, although I was innocent of any sin against her. At the weekend, I cycled into the square just as the whole family was climbing into their old Peugeot. Mr. Idrissi was looking like a good Muslim, wearing an immaculate cream-colored djellaba and a white tagia on his head. He merely gave me a wave and called out a polite "La bes?" How's everything?

In the safety of my house, I saw the funny side, relieved that things were back to normal in the square, and that Mr. Idrissi's pride had not been too badly bruised.

A Day in the Courthouse

Cristina was a Spanish friend, a nervous, slim girl with a head of frizzy ash blond hair. She was the youngest of eight sisters, a sculptor who had come on a visit to Marrakesh some five years before and had immediately recognized the home she'd been searching for. Inspired by her surroundings, she was the first to make the fashionable goatskin lamps that are decorated with henna by local women.

When Cristina moved from her apartment in Semlalia, she left behind a good deal of the plants she had grown on her terrace and told me I could have them if I wanted. She even told the landlady which day and time I'd come by to pick them up.

I arrived at the spiffy modern villa and rang the bell. There was no answer, so I waited in the street outside. Ten minutes later, a car appeared, was parked, and a hefty-looking woman in a brown dress got out. She must have known who I was, but she wouldn't look at me. I moved towards her to introduce myself: "I'm Cristina's friend. I've come for her plants."

"Hm," she snorted. "Well, we threw a lot out, there's only a couple left," she added haughtily, opening the gate and walking towards her house, as if dismissing me.

"Could I have them?" I asked politely, moving after her.

"No," she said, curtly. "She left the place in a mess."

"I don't think that's got anything to do with me or the plants," I began, but she interrupted me, taking me by the arm and steering me back towards the gate.

"Please go," she insisted.

It all happened very fast, but I decided I disliked the woman very much - her refusal to keep her word, her pushing me - and in a moment's fury, I found myself slapping her face. In an instant, the woman turned into a lunging bull, hurtling me out of the gate and across the street where she spread me over a stationary car, knocking my sunglasses off my head, and all the while yelling a torrent of insults at me in Arabic. I managed to extricate myself with a mighty shove, and beat a hasty retreat down the street, aware of an old house *guardien* staring incredulously at us from the doorway of a neighbouring villa. There had been a witness to the skirmish.

A few days later, I received a summons at the restaurant; if my exact address was never known in Marrakesh, it was well known I worked there. I duly presented myself at the Commissariat de Police on the date indicated. There, in a bare room, at a metal table, I made my statement to a police officer, who typed it as I spoke, one finger at a time, on an old manual typewriter. It took him a long time, time in which my imagination ran riot, recalling gruesome stories about people being detained by police in foreign countries. Police officers came and went in the corridor outside the room, eyeing me curiously, probably wondering what the normal looking foreign woman was doing there.

"You know that the woman is the wife of a Police Commissioner," the officer told me offhandedly when he was done. I tried not to show my ghastly shock at this revelation, and left the police station feeling very small and very anxious after he'd explained that I'd receive a court date in due course.

Not long after, the notice arrived. I wondered how to dress for the occasion – should I look elegant and rich, or plain and poor? As it was fall, I wore the only coat I had, which was an orange three-quarter length coat. I fixed my hair in a neat twist and wore low heels. Respectable was the look. In the courtroom, I found myself among a crowd of vociferous farmers wearing brown wool capes. They had come in from the countryside to settle disputes over water supplies, land problems and petty thefts of grain and sheep. I was the only woman, and needless to say, the only foreigner in the room, so I sat down on a bench and tried to make myself inconspicuous, while I waited for the court session to begin. Having never been in a court before, let alone a Moroccan one, I had no idea what I was waiting for.

Soon, three forbidding looking gentlemen in black robes with green satin sashes entered the courtroom and sat down in the Judges' seats. In front of the high imposing bench were some other men, whom I could only suppose were the prosecutors and defenders. The farmers argued their complaints, or defended their sins, and it seemed hours passed before I heard what sounded like my name being called. I stood up, trying not to look scared. Innocent, vulnerable, even lost would be all right, not scared. A man came towards me and led me before the Judges; presumably he was my defence counsel. They read out my crime in Arabic, and the man asked me in French if I was guilty of the charge. He also told me it was not permitted to speak to the Judges in any language except Arabic. I replied to the man in French and said yes, but that there'd been a good reason, which he then translated to the Judges. As there'd been a witness and the woman was the wife of a commissioner I could hardly deny it.

When my guilty plea was heard in the courtroom, there was a stunned hush and more than a few eyebrows were raised in surprise. I kept my eyes on the Judges to gauge their reaction, but they gave no sign of shock, condemnation or sympathy. They merely dismissed me. All the time I'd been praying it wouldn't be to jail, so I was glad to hear the man say I'd have to pay a fine, that the case would be marked on my alien file and that I'd have to see Le Procureur du Roi. This sounded a bit like the Spanish Inquisition, so I didn't much relish the idea.

Later, when I recounted the court scene to the Moroccan man I was seeing, he looked dumbfounded. "Why did you admit it?" he asked, shaken. For him, it was a matter of pride, and in admitting my guilt I had lost mine. "What is not seen has not happened," he said, uttering a fact I had by then encountered too often for my liking. I reminded him of the *guardien*, but he just shrugged.

A week or so later I received the notice to present myself to Le Procureur. An officer took me to the Tribunal in a police van, in which I sat feeling both ridiculous and ashamed. The Procureur's offices were in a building near Bab Doukkala and resembled those in a Franz Kafka novel: endless bleak corridors and rooms in which clerks sat at large desks heaped with dog-eared files. I sat on a hard bench and waited a long time, and then was asked to move to another hard bench in another long corridor.

Finally, I was shown into Le Procureur's grandiose quarters. "Bonjour, Monsieur," I managed to say, with a wan smile, from one end of the huge office.

"Entrez, Madame. Asseyez-vous," he said, not looking up from the document he was reading. "C'est grave," he said what I had done was grave.

"Yes, Sir, but she was very rude and pushed me," I said firmly.

"Maybe, but you can't take the law into your own hands. You should have filed a complaint," he admonished me.

"Yes, Sir," I replied. At that point, I got up from my chair and walked towards his desk. "I like living in Marrakesh very much," I began, "but sometimes it's hard," I said. "Would you please not mark my file because I want to go on living here?"

"She wanted to teach you a lesson," is all Le Procureur would say before dismissing me from his sight and his office.

I never heard anything more about the affair, and never received a notice to pay a fine. I spoke to a lawyer about the case one day; he said he'd look into it for me. When I saw him again, he said there was no record of a fine, nor was there any mention in my alien file. After that, my life in Marrakesh returned to normal. Although in truth, my life in Marrakesh was never normal.

ABDELSLAM: THE FASSI

One evening, on late duty in the lobby of the Sheraton Hotel where I had found employment after leaving the Moroccan restaurant, I found myself alone with Abdelslam. Of all the employees, he looked the least Moroccan, fair in skin tone, with fine straight brown hair and light brown eyes. Milder too in his speech and manners than most Moroccans, I took him for a European. I noticed him often at his work in reservations, where he went very earnestly about his tasks, and though he could take a joke like the rest of them, he wasn't one for talking much. I had also noticed that he would quietly disappear into a room set aside for the Muslim's five daily prayers.

That evening, I was feeling lonely and in need of comfort, and managed to engage him in conversation by relating some of my experiences in Marrakesh. To my surprise, I discovered a man of great faith. There was wholesomeness in the way he described his practice, from which he clearly derived joy and peace of mind. He had never before mentioned these things and did not now press them on me, so I found myself listening, quite entranced, as he told me how he had come to such faith.

He was born in Fès, of a father who was both a fakir and a bazaarist. "My father was a religious man, a scholar, and a good businessman too," he began, his eyes lit up with nostalgic affection. "Every evening over dinner, he would talk to us all – we were six children – about everything under the sun. He would bring out his great old volumes of learning and read to us, and would question us about all manner of subjects, and we would ask him questions," he went on, savouring his memories. "He told us about the Pyramids and the Pharaohs, about Mesopotamia and its far-reaching sciences."

I could see that from those evenings his imagination had caught fire, and had never ceased to burn. And then he described to me the time his father went on his first Hadj, the pilgrimage to Mecca.

"We had a big mansion house in the Medina of Fès. And in the house, we had everything we needed. On the roof, there were pigeons and chickens to eat, and to also give us eggs. There was salted meat hanging from a hook in the courtyard, there were bags of flour, couscous, sugar, spices, almonds and walnuts, and blocks of salt, and dates hanging in dark rooms, and our own water pumped from the mountains." I listened, amazed that this modern-looking man had grown up in such medieval surroundings.

"Do you know what my father did when he went on the Hadj?" he asked, his eyes shining with the anticipation of telling me. "He took the key to the only door of the house and locked it, so we would all remain inside while he was away!" I shook my head in disbelief as he continued. "There was a maid to help my mother. We had our own hammam, and our books to read and study, so he felt we were safe and had everything we needed until he returned. My mother never went out of the house anyway; the men did the shopping. She could only look out from the small high windows in the exterior walls of the house. That was the custom then. She accepted what my father did without question."

"And how long was he away?" I asked.

"In those days, the pilgrimage took about two or three months," he replied. "Of course, today it only takes a couple of weeks."

I had needed comforting, and had found it quite unexpectedly in talking to Abdelslam. That people could live with such faith, so resolutely going about their life the way they saw best, touched and inspired me. The father had given much to his son, a great respect, trust, faith, self-reliance, and a yearning for knowledge.

I never had another conversation like that with Abdelslam while I worked at the Hotel, but his presence, his smile and sense of well-being were a constant reminder that beneath the mask of daily life, everyone has a story to tell.

A Neighbourhood Exorcism

I lived a quiet life in Arsat el Hamid for a year or so. The only exception was the family with the renegade son, who was a law unto himself. Swarthy and rough round the edges, he always dressed in black and drove a truck for a living. The stocky ebony-haired mother also had a daughter, a teenaged version of herself who was always jumping on or off her boyfriend's moped. I never saw a sign of the father.

One morning, up to my elbows in laundry, I heard a loud commotion outside; women's voices, a lot of moaning and wailing. Familiar by then with the Moroccan's bent for fiery outbursts, I carried on, thinking it would pass. But it didn't; it went on and on. Finally, I went out into the square and saw that the boisterous family's door was wide open, and a group of women were staring in. Others came out, throwing their arms in the air, talking loudly, with much hand wringing. They were all so distraught that when I went over and entered the house, they paid me no attention at all.

Once inside, I stopped in my tracks. The daughter stood naked except for her underwear, which was drenched with water. Her long brown hair was hanging in sodden rats' tails. She was raving and shouting, over and over, "Shay haja fi rasi," there's something in my head. Her mother was throwing buckets of cold water over her. But it didn't stop her; she just kept tearing at her hair, her eyes rolling in her head, throwing herself around the room as if fleeing a demon.

The women were obviously at their wits' end and looked at me blankly, so I went up to the girl and took her by the arms.

"What is in your head?" I asked in Arabic, looking her straight in the eyes, thinking that the sight of a foreign face might shock her out of it.

But she just kept on screaming, "There's something in my head!" And her mother kept on throwing water at her.

Suddenly, I felt a presence behind me and looked back to the doorway. An old man wearing a yellow damask turban and black robe was looking in at the girl. He said nothing, his face expressionless, and then he was gone again. After a while, another man arrived and walked straight in. The women immediately stood back. He was a fakir. He wore a pure white turban and robe and carried a small bundle in a knotted handkerchief. Fakirs are consulted for matters ranging from exorcism, herbal remedies, faith healing and religious counselling, to finding a lost object. They also write magic charms called tilsam, or talisman.

"Dress her!" the fakir ordered, turning his back on the naked girl. She resisted violently, as the women struggled to take off her wet underwear and wrap a robe around her. When they were done, the fakir took the girl firmly by the arms, led her into the back room and pressed on her shoulders so she'd sit down. Then he pushed her back so that she was lying on the divan, took a blanket and tucked her in tightly to stop her writhing. While the girl kept shouting, the fakir put one hand on her head and chanted holy words, all the while anointing her forehead with holy water from the long spout of a glass bottle.

We stood around, speechless in the presence of the fakir, holding our breath as he slowly pacified the girl. At first she tossed and writhed, and then gradually she stopped. Her eyes began to close, but the fakir kept up his chants and his anointing until she was fast asleep. I left the house and went home, thinking about the things that lay beneath the daily round, and could appear without warning to haunt our days and nights. Demons, perhaps? Or the expression of the evil we feel around us?

A Session with
the Shiwofa

When I lived in Agadir, Hafida and Fatima had blushed and tittered nervously when they told me about s'hour, the magic charms cast by the outlawed shiwofa.

"They can make a man desire a woman, or detest her. They put things in food. They cast spells and hide them in the house. They slaughter chickens and leave them outside the door," the girls said, out of earshot of their devout mother, and bursting with a mixture of dread and excitement. "Maids are the worst," they said, "because they're inside your house, and can get their own back."

The sisters also told me about khait zinadi, which apparently was the good magic, the one that "undid" the bad magic. That was where the fakirs came in.

Now here I was, sitting with a shiwofa in her humble dwelling, in a small room on the slant that smelled of incense. We sat on the wooden floor, on a threadbare rug. The woman had thinning henna-dyed hair and very few teeth left, but spoke in surprisingly decent French when she asked me why I had come.

"There's a woman," I began, suddenly feeling I was on a wild goose chase.

"Ah," she smiled knowingly. "You think she is trying to take your husband?" I felt very foolish all of a sudden, but nodded.

"He's not my husband, but yes," I said, "I want to know if they have been lovers."

The shiwofa shuffled the primitive tarot-like cards. She cut them, set them down and told me to cut them again, after which she set them out in columns and stared hard at them.

"I see a dark man who loves you…" she began, like any clairvoyant anywhere.

I don't remember the rest of her musings about what she saw, the dark man, a jealous woman, but I remember she decided to use another method of divination. She took recourse to the Koran, opened the big tattered volume at random, and muttered aloud the verse she'd come upon. After this, she took a piece of glass hung on a thread and set to concentrating on how it swung. "If it goes back and forth, they did not. If it goes side to side, they did," she said. I watched like a hawk, in spite of misgivings about asking a strange woman about my life. The glass swung back and forth, but I was not convinced.

"If you want to make him stay with you…look only at you," she said, looking me straight in the eyes. "We can do something else." She hesitated then, to gauge my reaction; aware this was unknown territory for a foreigner. My curiosity got the better of me. "You must bring me some of his semen. You put it in your underwear and wear it for seven days. Each day, we will burn incense at sunset and speak the spell, and…"

For a brief moment, I found myself fascinated by the idea of such power, of putting it to the test. But when I thought of the man in question, of how I would manage to do it, I realized how absurd it was. "That's fine. How much do I owe you?" I said, shaking my head in disbelief that I had gone so far.

My session with the shiwofa cost me thirty dirhams; a few pennies that reminded me sharply of the dark tunnel of the imagination when it is let loose. As I left her house, I saw a dark young woman slip into the shadows in a nearby doorway, a modern Moroccan with lipstick and high heels who also wanted to maintain her anonymity while she reached out for help from the ancient ways of magic.

HEALING MY FOOT

"José lives by the mausoleum of Sidi Bel Abbès," Cristina said, as she led me to his house one torpid mid-summer afternoon. "His mother-in-law is a healer. Perhaps she will look at your foot." The big toe on my right foot had developed a sharp pain in the last week or so, and was causing me to limp.

As we approached the quartier where José lived, we were on sacred ground. We passed first through an immense walled-in square where a number of blind men were sitting in a circle chanting, begging for alms. "Allah! Allah!" they repeated over and over in a slow, persistent tone, holding out their small tins for coins. Around them a crowd of women had gathered; one had a newborn baby strapped to her deformed back, another, a dwarf, bore a baby half her size swaddled tightly behind her. They were all waiting to receive the blind men's blessings. Others were reading tarot cards, or burning metal to read fortunes in the melted twisted shapes. Rusted padlocks were attached to the outer grille of the mausoleum's enclosure, a way to leave worries to be healed by the Sufi saint, whose remains lay inside it. We left our shoes at the doorway and stepped barefoot into the empty musty mausoleum. In the presence of the long-bearded caretaker, we stood for a minute staring at the raised tomb and at the sombre vaulted ceiling that was draped in ancient cobwebs, left there to absorb the Saint's baraka.

Sobered by our visit, we crossed the square and went through a Moorish arch, entering a warren of tunnel-like alleys covered with wattle and eucalyptus beams. We were in a cool and darkened medieval labyrinth, crammed full of interlocking houses with slanting, crumbling walls and over-hangings that made us stoop the further in we went. It was always a surprise to see men emerge from the doorways wearing modern western clothes, out of place and out of time with their environment. As with everything, it was the women who kept up the old traditions.

Cristina stopped at a thick wooden door, worn with the ages it had seen, and rapped loudly. Voices were raised within the house, high-pitched and melodic, calling out to one another. A pretty young woman with radiant olive skin and thick wavy tresses opened the door with an "Ola!" and warm kisses on our cheeks.

Through a gloomy entrance lined with bicycles, we came into a tiled courtyard with potted plants in one corner, and a low round table and square rush stools in another. The courtyard was open to the cloudless cornflower-blue sky, and was overlooked by balconies dripping with the tendrils of lush green plants that fell in all directions. Two more girls appeared from a side room, younger, but with similar features to the first, and with the same manes of luxuriant dark hair. They wore sleeveless caftans in pink and violet, and embroidered velvet slippers. They flurried around us, full of excitement and curiosity. The one who had let us in was Najet, José's wife; the others were her sisters, Fatima and Zoubida.

"José met Najet ten years ago. They fell in love and he agreed to become a Muslim – they call him Abdelmoumen now – so they could marry. They have a little boy," Cristina explained. "José bought this house for them, but then the whole family moved in from the countryside," she whispered, grinning. "Suddenly, he found himself in the bosom of a large Berber family!" she went on, just as a man's voice called out from high up in the house.

"Cristina! Como esta?" Footsteps rang out as he descended the many flights of stone stairs. "I was practicing yoga," he said, coming over to kiss us both. José was a small, agile man with pale skin, kind blue eyes and wispy brown hair.

He organized a rug for us all to sit on, out of the scorching afternoon sun. I sat listening and watching as they all caught up on gossip in the Spanish José had taught them, which I do not speak.

"How long have you been in Marrakesh?" José turned towards me, and we spoke a little in English about how our paths had brought us there. He was young when he took leave of his bourgeois Spanish family to wander the world in search of things more soulful. His journey had taken him to South America and to India, where he'd stayed awhile to study Hatha yoga. After India, he had found his way to Morocco where he married Najet.

A few minutes later, a woman came towards us from the kitchen. It was Latifa, the matriarch, short in height, with tawny skin, a vision of skirts, scarf and apron in vivid orange and yellow. José got up and put his arm around her shoulders. "Latifa, la bes?" he asked how she was, as if he hadn't seen her for a long time. She grasped me firmly by the arms and kissed me, smiling shyly to display two gold-crowned teeth that matched her gold earrings. The hair that peeked out of her scarf was jet-black and glossy.

"Atay," she said, returning to her kitchen. While she was preparing the tea, I asked where the father was. He was in the country working his land. He got up every morning at four o'clock to go there, and didn't return until after dark. Latifa returned with the tea, which she served from a tin teapot shaped like Aladdin's lamp. She smiled constantly, nodding, as if the simple task made her happy. As we were sipping from dainty green glasses, Cristina remembered my foot and mentioned it to José.

"Ah, I will ask Latifa to look at it," he said. "Her father was a fakir. She inherited his gift," he added, walking over to the kitchen.

Latifa was turning hot couscous grains in readiness for dinner, but acknowledged José's request with a nod. She rinsed her hands and called out "Aji" to me, taking me first to the bathroom to wash my feet, and then to one of the salons where she drew back the drapes for me to enter. The small rectangular room was simply furnished with the usual divans on its three walls, a small round table, no ornaments or clutter. Muted sunlight flowed through the slats of the window shutters. Latifa told me to lie down, placed my foot on her lap, resting it on one hand, and with the other hand she began to gently feel all around my toe. "Qdim," she said the wound was old. She was right; I had forgotten a fall years ago. She probed and massaged my toe, gradually increasing the pressure until she reached the exact spot

101

where the pain was strongest. I winced but lay still with my eyes closed, trusting her, imagining her kind face and breathing regularly through the pain, while her hands continued their work.

After a half hour or so the pain decreased and I almost fell asleep it felt so good. When she stopped, I opened my eyes and began wriggling my toe, grinning with surprise.

"Chokran," I said, standing up and walking a few steps. My foot felt light and I could bend my toe without pain. "Cristina, José!" I called out. "My foot's better!"

José came into the salon. "You must give her a dirham as a token, because she cannot accept money for her gift," he said. I placed a coin in her palm, wishing I could have given more.

By the time the sisters brought the couscous to the table, José's son and the girls' young brother, who'd both been at school, had come home and nine of us sat down to eat. The meal tasted especially delicious, made as it was with such careful hands. I felt a great sense of pleasure and peace in the house, and a sense of belonging.

After a glass or two of fragrant verbena tea, Cristina and I took leave of the Berber Spanish family. José told me to visit whenever I wanted, for couscous or for yoga. On the way home, we passed through the same alleys of the Medina, only this time I felt like a Lazarus who had miraculously got up and walked, full of gratitude for the company, the food and the healing of my foot.

THE DAYS OF RAMADAN

It was the seventh or eighth day of Ramadan and the rhythm of daily life had undergone its annual change. In the daytime, it is not so much visible as something felt in the air. In the evening, it's the reverse: everything bursts into life, into gaiety and celebration.

The course of the day is topsy-turvy; fasting begins at dawn, "at the moment when a black thread can no longer be distinguished from a white one." Then, it's broken at sundown, anywhere from twelve to fourteen hours later, depending on the time of year, and is celebrated with the hearty ftour, 'breakfast.' The evening is for going out in the streets, for buying the special honey cakes, and for visiting family and friends. The ftour is followed later in the evening by a snack, the equivalent of 'lunch,' and then by 'dinner' sometime before dawn. Sleep is fitted in between 'lunch' and 'dinner,' or during the day for those who are able. Otherwise, you simply go about your business more slowly and quietly in the daytime. After twenty–eight days of this, it's not surprising that tempers are often frayed.

I was sitting on a hard, torn plastic seat in a Satas bus, which bumped along on one of those roads, full of sharp twists and turns that thread doggedly through the mountainous countryside, and stopped at every remote hamlet and forsaken outpost. The bus was full of cheery country folk returning to their bled, and the roof was packed high with sacks of flour, trussed chickens and sundry household items. In a trance-like state, I sat watching the shadow of the bus flit by on the rocky roadside banks, and held my breath when we careened down the mountain slopes.

It was late afternoon, and the ragged curtains did little to stave off the heat and glare of the sun that blasted against the windows. My head and hair were baking hot and I was perspiring against the hard plastic seat.

My thoughts turned to the day before, when I had cycled to have tea with Anne, a French friend, to talk about the man I was seeing. She had a Moroccan boyfriend too, and understood. I had left her house just after the muezzin had proclaimed the end of the day's fast, and found myself utterly alone in abandoned streets. The entire population simply disappeared. Not a soul was on the sidewalks, no cars moved in the streets, no motorcycles, not even a bicycle or a mule; every soul was in their home (or in someone else's) breaking the fast. As I cycled home on a short cut through residential neighbourhoods, I felt as if I were travelling through a ghost town, as if I were the only human left on the planet. I had never felt so lonely, anywhere in the world, as at that moment.

Now, in the bus, a clear, taped a capella voice intoned verses of the Koran, keeping a meditative Ramadan vigil for our journey. When the sun set, orange and blindingly brilliant, it cast its last rays through the imperious mountain peaks until it sank gently behind them and darkness enveloped the bus and the landscape. Before long, a flurry of blurred lights appeared ahead on either side of the road, and the bus began to slow down. The sun had officially set, it was time to break the fast.

The driver pulled in at a series of roughly built pink-painted arcades that were home to grocery stores, butchers' stalls and cafés. Kerosene lamps hung everywhere, and the smoke from charcoal grills filled the air. I stayed put as all the passengers roused themselves and filed off the bus, each to the café of his choice, to eat what he wanted. I had breakfasted around eight o'clock that morning, well after they had, and although I'd had no lunch, I wasn't hungry. I still had a heavy heart on account of the Moroccan man. So I sat watching from the bus as the others devoured plates of grilled meats with great gusto, washed down by mint tea and coffee.

When the bus horn signalled it was time to be off, the passengers returned to their seats. They were talking more now, no longer burdened with piety and hunger. A boy of about twelve or thirteen, wearing a shabby striped gandora, stopped at my seat. I looked up as he reached out his hands to offer me a carton of strawberry drinking yogurt and a hunk of flatbread filled with a mashed boiled egg. "Tiens, Madame," he said so humbly I couldn't find words to reply. I was caught between tears of sadness and tears of joy as I accepted the food.

"Chokran, wildi," thank you my son, I said, smiling with gratitude. I thought about the money he had spent on me, and was torn with indecision about whether to offer it to him or accept his kindness with grace so as not to insult him. The boy made up my mind for me. He simply smiled and sat down in his seat again, as though it was nothing, as though anyone would have done the same. For him, it was unthinkable to eat while others did not.

I ate the food he gave me with a burst of appetite as the bus raced on through the now invisible countryside to its final destination.

The most arresting moment of Ramadan comes surely on the last day, at the end of the old moon's cycle, at the sighting of the sliver of new moon. It follows the eve of the twenty-seventh day of Ramadan, Night of Power and Grandeur. In a wide sandy square, by the half-crumbling southern ramparts of Marrakesh, a thousand men must have been standing; all, rich and poor alike, were dressed in pure unblemished white. White djellabas with hoods, white turbans and tagia skullcaps, white socks and white babouche slippers. They stood shoulder to shoulder in dense rows, and then prostrated themselves simultaneously on the ground, while a low intonation echoed around and in through the windows of the bus in which I was travelling.

A couple of months after Ramadan falls Aïd el Kebir, the moment when a sheep is slaughtered in celebration of Abraham's faith in the Almighty. Not only do all the pilgrims in Mecca slaughter a sheep, but every Muslim family everywhere in the world. If you knew nothing of this, you would wonder why every village, hamlet, town or city suddenly had a host of sheep in its midst. I heard them bleating on rooftops in the Medina, and in front yards and behind the garden walls of modern villas in Gueliz. They would be bleating too as they lay draped across the handlebars of motorcycles, being transported – all dignity gone – from a country market through the traffic and pandemonium of the city, to the proud owner's home. To fatten the animals for the day of sacrifice, resourceful country folk brought in mounds of grasses to sell, setting them on any available space beside the road.

Like most foreigners, I dreaded the advent of the day itself. The number of sheep slaughtered at one time didn't bear thinking about. That mutton and lamb were scarce, expensive or even impossible to find after the sacrifice, changed nothing.

An ominous lull hung like a grey cloud in the sky from daybreak onwards, and the warm stale stench of sheep's blood lingered in the air all day. When I walked through the streets after the slaughter, rivulets of dark red blood mixed with water seeped from beneath doorways and gates everywhere, filling the gutters with streams that flowed in every direction.

One Aïd morning, having managed until then to forget the day of sacrifice, there came a knock at my door. A young boy stood there. "Besoin tuer le mouton?" he asked if I needed someone to slaughter my sheep. "Mon père," he added, pointing across the square.

Slaughtering was a man's job, handed down from grandfather to father to son. The King himself performed the act before his subjects, televised each year, to set the example. Their faith in this day was so all-encompassing it included the possibility of a foreign woman living alone and having a sheep that, as a woman, she was not permitted to slaughter.

"Merci, non," I replied, with a bit of a smile, not wanting him to read anything into my refusal.

Charcoal fires were lit in every home following the sacrifice, and the smoke wafted into every corner of Marrakesh, bringing with it the pungent smell of fat and seared flesh. Other fires were lit on the same roadside verges where the grasses had been, and severed sheep heads were hung in buckets over them to burn off the hide and hairs, before the head was steamed for hours indoors. I sat many times with neighbours, invited for the first of the many feasts at which the various parts of the sheep are eaten in ritual succession, all of us in a circle around the bowl in which the head took pride of place, picking at the tender cheeks and ears.

I took a certain secret pleasure, feeling like a heathen, far from eyes that would boggle in surprise and distaste, when I joined in with the spirit of things, with the community of people I lived among.

A Marriage Proposal in
the Kasbah

We were in a country bus, on the road that leads down from Ouarzazate to the date-palm oasis of Zagora, and had started out early to stay ahead of the stifling mid-day heat. The road winds up and over an unforgiving lunar landscape that glints with greenish metals, where few people live and where each mile seems to take you further away from civilization and further back in time. Here, the presence of a man seems no more significant than that of a tree or an animal – all are shrunk in size by the sheer vastness of the landscape.

Simon, my elder son, a passionate landscape photographer, had come over to Morocco to take photographs for the tree book, and we had been wandering for days, like nomads, wherever our search took us. On this trip, it was date palms.

The sliver of road went on and on, cutting through the baked and burnished Djbel Sarhro range until, from high above the solitary market settlement of Agdz, the lush green valley of the River Drâa appeared in the distance, far below us. To the east of the oasis and the wide brown river, the grey Kissane Mountains rose up in soft vertical ridges like folded velvet.

The bus drove slowly along the valley, beside the dense green forest of palms that cleaves to the river for a hundred miles down to Zagora.

We welcomed the signs of life: the oasis dwellers at work beneath the canopy of palms in emerald-green plots of rye and wheat. We passed kasbahs, the mud-castles of extended families, and ksours, fortified tribal enclaves. Imposing, almost menacing in their powerful structure, some stood tall and intact and were still inhabited, marked with primitive tribal motifs, triangles and barley stalks. Others were deserted, collapsing from aridity and wind like sandcastles washed away with the tide. The bus let us off across the river in Zagora, by an inn fashioned like a miniature kasbah. Here we took rooms, ate a tasty lunch and rested from the long drive.

At dawn the next morning, stuffed into a grand taxi with the locals, we set off to visit one of the larger ksours we had passed the day before. The taxi stopped beside a wide compound in front of the ramparts. The ground was covered with stacks of flame-red palm branches. Beside them dates of all sizes and shades – brown, red, yellow and orange – were heaped inside large squares marked out by stones. Turbaned elders with hands and arms like wiry branches were overseeing the work, while a crew of youths carried boxes of dates to the edge of the road where they were stacked onto trucks and taken to market.

In the centre of the thick turreted ramparts was a huge archway that led inside the ksar. We hesitated to bluster right in; the ramparts had been built to keep strangers out. But I was eager to get up close to the palm trees, ask about their cultivation, photograph them and eat dates straight from the branch, so we struck off in the direction of a path that led behind the ksar into the palm grove. We hadn't gone far when a man in a worn brown burnoose appeared in front of us, accompanied by some young boys. I called out "Salaam wa'aleykum," to show we came in peace, and the man threw back the burnoose hood to reveal his face, holding out his hand.

"I am the M'qadam." He was the village chief; a solid man in his mid-forties with wide shoulders, short tightly curled black hair, and sun-blackened skin.

I asked if we could see the palm grove, telling him in my pidgin Arabic about our tree book. "Wakha," okay, the M'qadam said, loosening his jaw enough to smile. His intense dark eyes lit up as he beckoned us to follow, not in the direction of the grove but back towards the archway that led into the ksar. I knew this meant we were headed to his home for the unavoidable glass of tea. Protocol required that before any business could be done, you must first become acquainted with, or rather be interviewed by, the M'qadam.

We found ourselves in cool, dank darkness, looking down a long covered passageway about ten feet wide towards a faint ray of daylight. On each side, doors were set in the mud and straw walls, and each home shared walls with the next; it was like a huge honeycomb. We couldn't see more than five feet in front of us as the M'qadam led us deeper inside. By that time, we were surrounded by children of all ages, mostly impudent little boys harassing us for "bonbons, floos, stylos" – candies, money, pens – their universal plea. Dozens of hands grabbed at mine as I took out a couple of the ballpoint pens I always carried for them, while Simon split a pack of chewing gum that they ruthlessly fought over.

Here and there, other passages led off in different directions; a man on a donkey flitted past, a woman darted inside her dwelling at the sight of foreigners. The M'qadam stopped at a lopsided door and rapped on it with the crude iron knocker; a protective hand of Fatima. A robust young woman with dark dotted chin and forehead tattoos opened the door. We followed the M'qadam into a room with rafters of quartered palm trunks, divided with fat wooden joists that stood on the bare earth. The woman picked up a baby that was lying on a soiled pillow on a low wooden shelf. The infant was tiny, with ruddy skin and a shock of jet-black hair, and was swaddled in a cloth that gave off strong baby odours. A black substance had been pasted on its eyebrows. "Ain khaiba," against the evil eye, the mother said. I tried to imagine what her life was like, how she coped, for she had probably given birth right there in the earthen cubicle. She was proud, but I sensed anxiety, perhaps like any mother anywhere, because it was her first baby.

"Hodi," she told me to hold the little girl, offering her to me with hands patterned with brick-red henna, bringer of good luck. I was touched that she wanted me, an unknown woman, to congratulate her on giving birth, to love her child too. I held it for a moment, staring at the improvised diaper and simple shawl, and thought of our babies, smelling of talc and dressed in the latest baby fashions. What a great gulf between the two.

The M'qadam led us into another bare room that resembled a stall. He pulled a saffron-stained rug from a hook and set it on the hard ground. Simon went off to take some pictures of the ksar, leaving me with the M'qadam sitting beside me on the rug. While we waited for the tea to arrive, I asked him about the oasis, about his date palms, about their life. "How many date palms do you have?" I began.

"I myself have a thousand," he replied, resting an elbow on the ground. "But there are many thousands in the palm grove. They are almost all female, just a few male palms to fertilize them. I will show you later." With this, he moved closer.

"Where is your husband?" he asked, staring at me with his unfathomable black eyes, adding without pausing, "I am looking for another wife." From the intense way he looked at me, it was clear he saw me as a candidate. My first reaction was to brush the comment off with a laugh, but I stopped myself. We had after all walked into his life uninvited, and I must be polite. I pretended not to have understood and smiled a lot, praying the woman would return quickly with the tea.

Fortunately, she did. "Don't leave me again," I whispered to Simon when he came back. "The M'qadam was about to propose!"

With the tea ceremony over, the M'qadam took us out into daylight again. Through a thicket of towering trunks we found ourselves inside the palm grove, in the gardens that grow beneath the date palms' canopy. We walked beside the narrow irrigation channels, along a web of pathways edged with low mud walls, and could almost hear the vegetation growing. The M'qadam pointed out various palm trees and types of dates, sometimes walking so close I could feel his coarse burnoose against my bare arms. But he was kind and picked us dates from the branch to eat, and seemed proud of his land, patiently answering my incessant questions; some of which I posed to keep his mind off me.

Finally, he gave up the chase. The sun was now right above us, baking hot and blindingly bright. When I put on my sunglasses, the M'qadam took out his own pair – modern black wraparounds – that reminded me again how everyone in Morocco is a walking contradiction, blithely holding opposites in the palm of their hand.

On the way towards the fast-flowing River Drâa that irrigates the whole oasis, he stopped to greet men scaling the sharply spiked palm trunks, barefoot without any apparatus, and women weeding the plots or bearing bales of weeds, their backs bent double under the weight and width.

"The tribe that built the ksar grew so large we don't know anymore which one is family and which isn't," he chuckled, when I asked him about the origins of his people.

Our walk eventually brought us back to the archway. When we declined the M'qadam's invitation to stay for lunch, he looked quite disappointed. We stood on the roadside waving at him, clutching our cameras and note-pads and the branches of ripe sticky dates he had thrust in our arms, and waited for a grand taxi to take us back to Zagora.

Had the M'qadam just been dreaming, like we all do? Or in his reality, was the desire to marry a woman sufficient reason to ask? Did he think he could bring me into his tribe simply because he wanted to? I learned things about date palms and the people of the ksour that day, but about this I will never know.

Riding Low in a Country Bus

It was mid-afternoon in late October, still hot and dry. Simon and I had been staying in Taroudant with Swiss friends who managed Royal orange groves. We'd spent a week or two learning all about the oranges that grow in abundance in the region, and were now headed to Ouarzazate and date-palm country.

We were standing on the only paved road that leads out of town to points east, waiting for one of the rundown country buses or one of the beat-up 'grand taxis' that ferry locals about, or anything else with wheels going in our direction. No timetables, no reservations, potluck.

An hour or more had passed since our friends had waved us off. Bored with standing still on the deserted road, we began to walk, turning back now and again to see if anything was coming. When we began to sweat in the sun, we stopped again and stood back from the road in the shade of some eucalyptus trees, sloshing bottled water over our heads.

The bus seemed to appear from nowhere and we rushed forward to flag it down, shouting "Hey! Hey!" as loudly as we could. It sailed right past us and left us staring at its behind with our mouths wide open. But then, fifty or so yards ahead, it came to a screeching dust-cloud halt. Grabbing our back-packs, we ran as fast as we could in case the driver thought better and set off again. The door opened and the driver's mate stood there, frowning. "Pas de place," the mate said. The bus was full, all seats taken. "Gendarmes," police, he added, shaking his forefinger back and forth. We knew already they weren't allowed to let passengers stand, but we kept saying "Aufek," please, pleading with the mate and the driver, until, with a shrug of defeat, they let us climb aboard.

There, in the narrow aisle, we stood, holding on to the metal seat-backs as the bus careened along the road. The passengers were all swarthy country folk: men, women, youths and children; their cargo of chickens and bags and sacks of vegetables and flour gave off thick vegetative odours, liberally mixed with the sweat of their labours. They eyed us phlegmatically, while we, as usual, felt like aliens beamed down from a blond and blue-eyed planet.

We hadn't gone more than ten miles or so before the bus began to brake sharply. We looked ahead and saw the inevitable; a road block of gendarmes. The drivers' mate signalled frantically to us with a downwards hand movement, indicating that we should crouch down in the aisle. We obeyed, sank to our haunches, and kept our heads down, feeling like children playing hide-and-seek. The bemused dark eyes of the passengers, now our collaborators, were all upon us, watching for our reaction.

The bus came to a stop, the driver sat still, hoping he'd be waved on. But a grey-uniformed officer with a peaked cap and manicured moustache stepped quickly into the bus. Silence and fear reigned; everyone held their breath, knowing the severity of Moroccan police, as the officer sternly surveyed the situation. His glance immediately fell on us, still crouching. Caught in the act, we both sheepishly rose to our feet, keeping as straight-faced as we could, given the ridiculous circumstances. The whole bus was waiting for the officer's decision: would we have to get off, would the driver be fined?

The officer's steely eyes searched all round the bus, and alighted on two youths. He pointed at them, said something gruff in Arabic that we didn't understand, and the two youths promptly stood up and vacated their seats. The officer then pointed at us and at the seats, silently choreographing the change over. We thanked the young men, grinned, and dutifully sat down.

After a few admonishing words to the driver, without any ticket or money changing hands, the officer seemed satisfied that justice had been served and climbed out of the bus. He stood on the road beside his grey Jeep and waved the driver on with a broad authoritarian sweep of his arm. As we drove off, a wave of laughter exploded through the bus. And then we were rolling along again, all quiet and drowsy, except for the clucking chickens, as if nothing had happened. Except now the two young men were standing in the aisle instead of us. As for the officer, we thought he had probably enjoyed the whole thing too, and had chosen to display good public relations in front of foreigners.

A Litre of Olive Oil

Up in the north of Morocco, in the region around Fès and Meknès, grow the best olives because the soil and the climate are just what the olive trees need. It was a sunny warm Sunday in late October, the season for the olive harvest. Simon and I were once again on our tree quest, headed for Rafsai, a remote village in the heart of olive country, where we'd heard the villagers held a moussem to celebrate the harvest.

A thin winding road edged with giant agaves, led us through waves of barren beige and grey sandstone ridges, and then we came to a gentler landscape of hills and vales, thick with wild lavender and thyme, whose piquant fragrance filled the air. Finally, this gave way to immense green plateaus and valleys studded with olive trees. Set out in perfect rows that swooped up to the sky on the distant hills, the olive groves stood, as they have since time immemorial. Hardy to the extreme, if you cut one down to the trunk, just a foot or two from the ground, it regenerates to become even more bountiful. It is the Tree of Peace because it takes many undisturbed years to cultivate an olive grove.

As we motored on, we noticed in the corners of every grove, mountains of black olives, shiny and moist, seeping their juices onto the ground. Yellow plastic tents were staked beside the mounds so that caretakers could keep watch over them day and night. It was indeed harvest time.

We stopped at several hillside hamlets already busy with the oil-making . Each had a communal trough filled with freshly picked ripe black and purple olives. A team of mules plied round and round the trough, rotating a wooden lever attached to a huge circular stone that crushed the olives to a pulp. Dark purplish-brown stains oozed from the troughs and seeped down the hillsides like winding paths, leaving the pungent odour of olive oil hanging in the air. I asked many questions of the wiry weathered countrymen, while Simon photographed them at work. We watched as the thick oil ran from the baskets into a hollow carved in the ground, into which water was added to make the dark solids sink. Before we left, each farmer scooped a ladle of the golden-green oil for us to taste, proud of his produce and eager for our approval.

Some time later we drove into Rafsai. More a settlement than a village, it comprised a mixture of mud and stone houses, some with thatched roofs, some flat, strewn haphazardly beside the dusty tarmac road. It was a quiet, sleepy place with one store and a simple café-cum-hotel with a handpainted sign that proudly announced Hotel des Oliviers.

There were many eyes upon us as we stepped into the café and sat down. "Salaam wa'aleykum," I said, asking for two coffees. It was a Wild West scene, a long metal counter, and dusty men with noble faces and dark beard shadows, clothed in brown cloaks and burnooses so worn they looked like old sacks. Others sat idly at plastic tables, either watching a beat-up TV set or staring blankly at us. The coffee was espresso with steamed milk, and was particularly good; the kind of incongruity that never failed to surprise me. We sat for a while before disturbing them with our inquiries. When Simon asked for cigarettes from the man who seemed to be the café's owner, I asked him where the olive market was.

"Lioum" came the reply in Arabic; today. When is, of course, as important as where.

"Fin?" Where? I asked again. The man looked at me and laughed, acknowledging my presence as if I had appeared suddenly from nowhere.

"Just through the village, towards Ouezzane," he said, vacantly.

"And the moussem?" I went on.

"Ah," he carried on twisting the old espresso machine. "Last week," he replied.

"Is anyone still harvesting?" I asked, disappointed.

"Yes, a few farmers are late," he said, still deadpan.

When we had finished our coffee, we left the café with the man, whose curiosity had by that time gotten the better of him. If he was the café owner, he had no trouble leaving his establishment in the care of his patrons, who seemed to be installed there permanently, for want of something better to do. The man took us first to his brother's olive grove a few miles up the road. Simon went to photograph the young men up in the trees, who were prodding the branches with sticks to dislodge the olives. I joined the women in their bright floral skirts and scarves, and crouched down with them on a plastic sheet to sort the olives that were raining down from above. They asked no questions as to why we were there, but seemed greatly amused that we would want to photograph them and help at their harvest. I worked shoulder to shoulder with the women until the baskets were full of olives and my hands were stained a deep blackberry.

I had never thought before to taste a raw olive, but they looked so beautiful straight from the tree that I popped one into my mouth. I quickly spat it out; it was so bitter. The women burst into laughter and wagged their fingers at me. Who first thought olives would taste good if they were packed in salt, or steeped in oil? And that if they were crushed, they'd yield such a golden glory?

As it was the day for the weekly olive souk, the man came with us to show the way. We offered to drive him back to his café, but he shook his head and ambled off among the turbaned farmers who were deep in negotiations for the price of their olives. There wasn't a sign of modern civilization anywhere, just biblical-looking men, heaps of olives on raised wooden stands, crude scales and jar upon jar of olive oil. I butted in as politely as possible to ask the price of the olives and of the oil, and received either terse replies or stares. I clearly bewildered them, a blond foreign woman interrupting their solemn bargaining rituals. But others were more resourceful and quickly offered to sell us their oil. A pack of young men and boys followed us closely, idly passing their Sunday, edging into Simon's photo frames, grinning wide-eyed at the camera. Unlike the women, who always refused to be photographed, the men clearly got a thrill from posing.

Suddenly, engrossed in the goings-on, I lost sight of Simon. He was always easy to spot, blond among a race that had no blond men, but now he was nowhere to be seen. I searched all round me and then noticed a pair of soldiers in berets and fatigues about fifty yards away, beckoning, and walking towards me. I had an awful feeling we might be in trouble. The soldiers approached me and said to go with them. It didn't sound as if I had a choice, so I followed them in silence with a stiff small smile. While we had been watching the olive selling, we too had been watched.

We arrived at a hut in a grassy clearing. Simon was already sitting inside with a blank expression on his face that I gathered meant he didn't want to betray concern to the soldiers. There were two or three more soldiers in the hut.

"What happened?" I whispered.

"They told me to go with them," he said, flatly. One of the soldiers, seated at a table, asked what we were doing in the market.

"We are writing a book about the olive tree," I said, realizing how unlikely that must have seemed to him.

"Hm," was all he said, producing a form printed in Arabic and French which he began to fill out as he asked us questions, speaking in a mixture of both languages. "Fin tomobil?" he asked us first where our car was. Simon pointed. Then our names, our country, our jobs, our addresses, our ages, my mother's maiden name, where were we staying, were we married?

"No, he's my son," I explained, receiving baffled frowns. Simon is a tall strapping young man, and was about thirty-three at the time; hence their confusion. The list of questions seemed to have been taken from every bureaucratic form in the world. Meanwhile, I was hoping the worst wouldn't happen; that we'd be clapped in the local jail for reasons best known to them. The questions and form-filling went on for a long time while another man, a tall heavily built old man with thick loose robes and a voluminous bandage-like turban, sat looking at us, without saying a word. I guessed he was the sheikh of the local commune. We too sat there quietly waiting. There was an air of expectancy in the small hut; something was about to happen.

When a clean-shaven gentleman in his fifties, with spectacles and piercingly bright eyes, dressed in a spruce navy worsted suit, walked into the hut, all the soldiers and the old man stood up. There was much handshaking, nodding, and courteous "Salaam wa'aleykums." The gentleman was good enough to explain to us that he was the Caid of the region, a man under the governor, but superior to the Sheikh. He said he'd been sent for because there were foreigners at the olive market. He didn't say that they hadn't known what to do with us.

"Have you bought olive oil?" the Caid went on, politely.

"Yes," I replied, showing him the bottle into which one of the olive merchants had poured a liter of oil.

"And how much did you pay?" the Caid asked.

"Thirty dirhams," I replied, at which all the men in the hut looked solemnly at each other and at the Caid.

"Good, that is correct," the Caid said, nodding his approval. With that, he took the bottle from me, opened it and upturned it enough to let a few drops fall on his fingers. He tasted the oil, licked his lips, and nodded in approval again.

I had to explain again why we were at the market, about our book and wanting to know all about olives and olive oil, and as I did the Caid looked more and more pleased.

"Well, here is another litre," he said, offering us a large container. "It's from my own olive grove," he added getting up, finally satisfied that everything had been well understood and dealt with in his fiefdom.

GAMES WITH THE TOURISTS

We had been driving for many hours, motoring eastwards from Taroudant to Ouarzazate on a gruelling open and desolate road. Although it was spring and some greenery had sprung up here and there on the otherwise barren landscape, we were not far from the Sahara and the temperature was nigh unbearable.

About forty kilometres from our destination, we noticed a car some hundred feet ahead, pulled over on the narrow hard shoulder. Two men were bent over the engine, shaded by the car's hood. They looked up as we approached and one of them, his shirtsleeves rolled up and his hands oil-stained, stepped out into the middle of the road, waving frantically. He looked like a decent working-class man, but having by then seen the whole gamut of tricks played on tourists to part them from their money, I sensed something afoot. We weren't in the mood for any tomfoolery and our hotel, with its showers and comfortable beds, was too attractive a prospect to waste time getting there.

My first thought was to tell Simon to drive on, but a small voice inside stopped me. I imagined myself stuck in the middle of nowhere, in that heat, and so we came to a stop right where the man stood.

"We have been trying to fix it for hours…" he began, an imploring look on his sweat-beaded face. "All I need is for you to take a note to my brother in Ouarzazate, and he will come to help." He ran over to his car and returned with a note, neatly written in Arabic script. There was even a map on the back. It had to be a set up. I could have handed the note back and driven away, but there was that last iota of doubt that wouldn't let me, so I said, "OK, we'll take it." It wouldn't cost us any extra time or money, and my conscience would be clear.

When he saw that his plan seemed to be working, the man gave us a hesitant smile and thanked us several times as we drove away. In the rear mirror, I watched him return to his companion, who was still tinkering under the car's hood. As we neared Ouarzazate, we followed the map and duly arrived at the gas station indicated. In our white Fiat Uno, a common rental for tourists, the alleged brother spotted us instantly as we pulled in. He looked nothing like a garage mechanic. He was dressed like a Blue Man in the traditional long indigo robe and navy-blue turban – a common ploy to charm tourists. I wasn't fooled.

"He's no more a Blue Man than you are!" I said gruffly to Simon, who finally gave way to laughter.

"It didn't do any harm," he said, shrugging.

The man walked over and I waited to see what he'd say, like how much gas did we want? But he just smiled at us and said nothing, so I presented him with the note. He read it and smiled again. "Thank you," he said. "I will send someone to them now." I nodded to the man, which Simon took as his cue to drive off. But the man leaned quickly forward, resting a hand on the open car window, and said, "You have been so kind, I would like to invite you in for tea."

At this point, Simon, now more inclined towards the gin and tonic he would order once we arrived at the hotel, said firmly: "La chokran, sidi," no thank you sir, as he drove away, leaving the Blue Man standing against a gas pump, looking perplexed.

A few days later, we were in Zagora, on the edge of the Sahara, sitting in a small café. Lunch was hamburger and fries, resourcefully adapted from the Moroccan version for the tourists and as we began to eat, a young couple sat down at the next table, the only other customers. They looked exhilarated and happy, but pale; evidently new arrivals not yet exposed to the sun. In the desert you are pleased to find comrades, as though having made it that far makes you one of the same tribe.

"Where are you going?" the young woman asked in French, as we pored over our Michelin map.

"Across to Rissani and Erfoud," I replied. "And you?"

"We're staying here for a day or two. We've just come from Ouarzazate," she said.

They were on their honeymoon and seemed thrilled with their choice of Morocco, as though it fulfilled a long-held fantasy. The husband told us about the things they'd seen and done, and remarked how friendly and hospitable the people had been. And then the woman stopped. "Shall we tell them?" she asked her husband, who thought for a moment and then said yes. "Well, we were not far from Ouarzazate when we came to a car broken down on the road," she began.

"I know," I stopped her. "They gave you a note with a map, and asked you to take it to a garage?" I went on. The couple looked surprised and embarrassed. "I knew it was a scam, but I took it anyway," I told them, and we all laughed a lot.

The couple had accepted the Blue Man's invitation to tea, of course, thinking it a nice gesture and a chance to get a glimpse of real life in Morocco. "He took us into a house, but it was like a carpet bazaar, full of rugs and carpets," the wife continued. I could guess what was coming.

"We bought a rug," she went on, looking puzzled. "We paid two thousand dirhams – it's nice but we didn't really want one."

"They asked me for my Nikes and my t-shirt too!" the husband added, grimacing.

"And you gave them to them?" Simon asked. The husband nodded slowly, clearly wondering how he could have been so gullible. When we parted company, I couldn't help wondering what they would make of it all when they were safely back home with the rug on their living-room floor.

VODKA WITH THE CAID

Soldiers in sludge-green uniforms stood by the sentry box at the iron gate of the Caidat in Tafraoute. The pink pisé walls that fronted the building were blanketed with fluffy yellow mimosa blossoms and made an unlikely setting. We walked up to the soldiers and asked to see the Caid, at which they shook themselves out of their mid-afternoon torpor and looked at each other, wondering what to do. One of them took it upon himself to make a decision and disappeared through a door set in a high wall that led into the grounds of a large mansion house, a relic of the French colonialists. A moment or two later the soldier returned, nodding officiously. "Le Caid arrive," he said, not letting us take another step forward. And then, from the same door, a man emerged and came sauntering towards us.

Handsome, with a sallow complexion, he seemed to be in his early fifties, and was dressed in a light cream-colored suit; in all, not what I expected of a Caid in a rough mountain village. Until the early part of the 20th century, Caids were often ruthless men who wielded immense power over the local Berber tribes. Times had changed, and luckily, our host was both hospitable and charming. As he approached, with the hint of a smile at his lips, he stretched out his arms in welcome as though we were long-lost friends.

"Entrez, Madame et Monsieur," he said, shaking our hands and leading the way to the house.

"I heard you were in town," he began, reminding me how word-of-mouth was faster in those parts than The Daily News.

We sat on the tiled veranda and looked out on a wild garden that sprawled its way around the house. Numerous tall ornamental palms had long ago been planted to shade the house and veranda from the south's implacable heat. A gardener wearing a dog-eared straw hat, pottered with the white opiate datura and pruned the scarlet hibiscus, while colonies of birds gossiped high up in the palm trees.

"It is my shame if you are not my guests," the Caid continued. "After tea, I will send Simon to your hotel with my driver to pick up your things. You will stay here," he finished, smiling at me. In spite of his gentle manner, it would be hard to argue with this man, I thought.

Half an hour later, the driver lugged our bags into the house. "Now we can talk," the Caid said looking quite excited. "I've asked my wife to prepare couscous tonight! With mutton," he added, thinking aloud as he imagined the meal.

I explained that we were in Tafraoute to write about the argan tree, and to find Najib's sister, Fatima, at work on the harvest and oil making. As she lived in the tiny remote village of Asguine, there had been no way of contacting her beforehand. The Caid quickly raised his arm in a flourish and said, "I will send you with my driver to look for her tomorrow." We thanked him for his generosity, and then, with me taking furious notes, he began to tell us all the facts and figures about the argan tree. He explained how crucial it was to the local economy, how the trees were disappearing fast, and spoke of the steps being taken nationally and internationally to protect the trees. He also spoke of the women who cultivated them.

When the sky began to darken, a woman came into the room.

"My wife," the Caid said, as though speaking of one of his staff. She was of medium height and voluptuous build, and her large black eyes stood out in contrast to a satin caftan the colour of cherries, beneath which the lace edges of white pantaloons peeped seductively. The woman nodded and smiled shyly at us, and then disappeared as quickly as she had come. The Caid disappeared too, leaving Simon and I alone for a moment to finally exchange whispers. A word or two went a long way, a short-hand we had invented so as not to rouse our host's suspicions. We had been whisked out of our own itinerary, vague as it was, and had become the captives of the Caid. In olden days in these regions, from what I'd read, as Christians, we might have been beheaded or left to rot in a dungeon.

"We have a nicer room now," Simon said, with a straight face. Just as I regained my composure, my ears registered music in the house, not Arabic music, but the smooth crooning voice of Frank Sinatra. The Caid came back into the room humming along, enjoining his voice to Frankie's chorus, I did it my way. "He is my favourite singer," he said, with a sigh.

As he lolled on the divan, hugging a cushion against his belly, the Caid seemed lost to a private reverie. "I had an American girlfriend once," he began. "Anyway, she went back to America, and I married this one," he stopped, apparently at a loss to explain his life. And then he reached beneath the divan and pulled out a bottle of Smirnoff vodka. "Time for a drink," he announced, calling out for glasses to be brought. His wife brought them to us on a tray and left again quickly, her eyes averted, as though not wanting to see the worst.

As we sipped our drinks, the Caid went over to an old TV in the corner of the room and we found ourselves watching a black and white John Wayne in Rio Bravo, speaking quite marvellously in fluent French. When the Caid noticed the bottle was empty, he said, "Simon, wildi. You must go to the Hotel Amandiers and buy us some more." Declining the hundred-dirham note he offered, Simon stood up and showed himself ready for the errand, although I knew he really wasn't. It was a long uphill haul to the Hotel, through overhanging boulders, and it was pitch-black now; but it was the least we could do. I couldn't help wondering who ran the errand for the Caid on other occasions, alcohol being forbidden to Muslims.

The couscous duly arrived, a huge steaming pyramid of meat and vegetables, and I struggled to make a dent in the part nearest me. By then, I was having a hard time just to keep my eyes open. Around midnight, the Caid rose and bade us goodnight. Our accommodations were in a high-ceilinged salon furnished with brocade divans, its walls hung with curved daggers and silver-encrusted muskets; a far cry from our cheap hotel. In the silence and darkness, it came to me who he reminded me of. It was Charles Aznevour: a melancholy man who, like the Caid, seemed out of place; a man who sang of love with a plaintive voice that could pierce your soul. The Caid was Moroccan; Aznevour, Armenian. I remember thinking we are all lost souls searching for our home and for love.

In Search of the
Argan Tree

I tasted argan oil long before I set eyes on the tree itself. Najib and his wife had served it at breakfast on my first morning in Morocco. Along with homemade bread, there had been a saucer of amber-tinted oil, light in texture, but rich, tangy and strongly nutty in flavour and aroma. As the argan trees grew in his native region, Najib described the tree and its oil with great enthusiasm. The story was so fascinating, and the oil so delicious, that I resolved to one day find out more.

And now here we were, bowling along in the Caid's Land Rover on a winding ribbon of road in the Ameln Valley, where the argan forest sprawls across a low-lying plain between mountains of pink granite and sand stone. We were in the heart of argan country. Above and around us, the steep slopes were covered with huge pink boulders balanced one on top of the other, all seeming ready to topple at any moment. Gingerbread hamlets emerged from the rock face between the boulders, blending in chameleon-like with their surroundings; others were nestled at the foot of the mountains, clustered around a spring.

The trees grow wild; their steely grey trunks twisted, gnarled and thorny. The foliage is thick and dense, sometimes dark green, sometimes lime green, on branches spread out like graceful canopies, the only shade anywhere to be seen. At a small hand-written sign, the driver turned sharply and in a haze of dust we bumped up a beaten track towards Asguine. Carpets of ripe brown argans surrounded the argan trees' trunks, and there were new green ones on the branches too, from this year's growth. Like large olives, some were oval in shape, others teardrop or tapered. And then suddenly, we noticed there were goats in some of the trees! They looked like mythical birds, perched some ten or fifteen feet up, clinging awkwardly to the branches with their forelegs as they chewed the aerial pasture of leaves and argans, their tongues and hides oblivious to the sharp thorns. The driver told us the goatherds were not supposed to let their animals graze the forest or climb the trees during harvest time, but I wondered what else they could eat as there was no grass at that time of year.

As we got closer to the hamlet, all appeared deserted. Most of the men had gone to the cities or abroad to earn their living, the driver told us. The Tafraoutis had become the tradesmen and grocers of Casablanca. They work hard and get rich, some take their families with them, but they always come back to their village to build new houses to retire in. Further on, a few scruffy young boys were jostling in the dirt. One of them held out a small chameleon, asking how much we'd pay. The forest is home to a large variety of wildlife – birds, hares and rabbits, honey badgers, Barbary squirrels, hedgehogs, snakes and scorpions. The driver asked the boys where we could find Fatima. They called out that she was with friends in Anamr, one of the villages further along the mountainside.

A few minutes later, we turned onto another track, but it soon became too steep and rocky for the Land Rover to negotiate, so we continued on foot. Irrigation channels ran through olive groves; alongside them, Barbary fig hedges were covered with their prickly yellow cactus fruits. The air echoed with the splashing of springs gushing between rocks, trickling downhill to the gardens, and with the sound of songbirds darting through the undergrowth. We came across a wrinkled old man sitting at a concrete water tank. It was his job to measure with his fingers against the side of the tank the amount of water each family received; the amount depending on the size of the family and of their land. We sat down on the wall beside him, in the shade, absorbing the peace. The driver asked him where Fatima was, and he pointed to a house standing on a craggy ledge, the highest in the hamlet.

The house was reached by a series of steep twisting steps carved from the earth, and as we began to climb, we heard a piercing voice and saw a woman in black peering down at us. "You came all this way to find me?" Fatima cried, clambering quickly down and embracing me warmly. She was short and solidly built, with chestnut hair and light blue eyes – an unusual sight in Morocco. We spoke in French and Arabic as she linked my arm in hers up the rest of the steps.

When we stood on the ledge by the house, surrounded by heaps of argans and oil making utensils, there was a panoramic view of the whole sun-drenched Valley. Three women, of three generations, were staring at us with quiet curiosity, averting their eyes from Simon. Swathed in shiny black cloths called tamelhafs, edged with multi-coloured ribbons and sparkling sequins, they were small in height, with intense black eyes and high, sculpted cheekbones. The youngest woman came to greet us and spoke only Soussi Berber. Her mother stayed shyly over by the very old grandmother who was sitting on the ground in the shade of some argan trees. Although she was wizened and crooked from a life of hard labour, the twinkle in her eyes made clear she hadn't yet given up to dying.

Inside, the cool mud home was a warren of bare rooms and earthen floors, with thick walls and narrow windows. Fatima prepared tea in a tiny dark kitchen and brought us a tray of bread, argan oil and amlou – a dip made of oil, almond butter and honey from honeycombs found in the argan trees. Argan oil is too strong for cooking, but is sometimes used to dress salads, Fatima told me. In the old days, before the arrival of gas cylinders, they used the oil for lighting too. It's a panacea, believed to have tonic and aphrodisiac qualities and is used medicinally, to heal acne and chickenpox scars and to relieve the pain of rheumatic joints. Fatima said the locals claim it can treat heart disease, and is thought to be good for the liver and gall bladder too. As a cosmetic, the women use it as massage oil, applying it to their nails to strengthen them, and to their hair as a tonic.

The rest of the day passed slowly. I sat on the ground beside the women, while they continued the arduous and time-consuming job of cracking the thousands of argans that had been drying in the sun. I watched as Fatima held a dried argan between finger and thumb against a large flat stone, and struck it sharply with a small smooth stone. When the argan split open, with a lightning turn of her wrist, she flicked it against the flat stone to release two small ivory kernels that resembled cantaloupe seeds. I tried doggedly to do the same, with much teasing, managing to crack a mere fifty and paying for my efforts with a red and swollen thumb.

Berbers are furiously resourceful, so when I looked at the heaps of cracked shells, Fatima immediately understood. "We waste nothing. They're for kindling. We make the argan flesh into mash-cake for the goats, sheep and camels and the solids from the oil-making provide patties for cows. It makes them strong, so they give more milk."

The trees vary so much in size it was hard for Fatima to say how much oil they yield, but a healthy full-grown tree gives about twenty baskets of argans, about two hundred pounds that produce just a litre of oil. It takes a woman a full day's cracking, grinding and kneading to produce that litre, which sells at the local souk for about eighty dirhams, or eight dollars. Fatima always sent a bottle to her mother, Khadija, and to Najib, who guard it like a treasure because it's hard to find in the cities, and is not always pure – unscrupulous vendors add cooking oil to eke it out and paprika to enhance its reddish-amber colour. According to Fatima, the test for pure oil is to place it in the refrigerator. If it gets thick and creamy looking, it's pure. If it stays liquid, it's not.

When the searing heat had eased and the mountains were turning dazzling pink and mauve in the oncoming sunset, Fatima offered to take us to her house in Asguine for the night, and to the harvest the following morning, with the whimsical warning, "We go out very early!"

Before we set off, the mother presented me with a small jar one quarter full of argan oil and I humbly accepted this prized possession, knowing now how many hours had gone into its making. I had nothing with me to give her in return and as the offer of money would have been an insult, I promised to write and send photos.

Fatima led us sure-footedly down the mountain slopes, stepping over rivulets, across jagged white rocks in a dried-up riverbed, and through thickets of shrubs and sapling argans. She halted for a hair-raising moment when she sensed the presence of wild boar, and then strode on relentlessly. By the time we were creeping through the argan trees and olive groves of Asguine, it was pitch black. Even so, Fatima could still pick out those trees that belonged to her family. Here and there, the shadowy form of a girl returning from the gardens dashed for cover behind a tree, like a startled animal; even in the dark, they hide themselves from men.

The hamlet was silent and cool, with not a soul in sight, but the air was thick with the smell of grass and mint, of animals and the warm aromas of cooking. The lower floor of Fatima's house was home to some chickens, a donkey, argan shells and dead argan branches that served as kindling, urns of water and jars of olives and olive oil. Uneven earth steps led to the upper floors, and we groped our way in the dark, stumbling, while Fatima flew up with agility. We followed her into a rustic room with a low wattle ceiling. There was no electricity, so she lit candles and a gas lamp. We brought water from the basement to wash vegetables, while Fatima cooked an omelette in a pan set over the burner of a small gas cylinder. Later, although I fretted a moment about insects, snakes and scorpions, I was so tired, and it was so blissfully quiet, I soon fell asleep.

In the early hours, I heard Fatima begin to move around, boiling water for ablutions before the dawn prayer. I watched for a while and then dozed again, until a singsong trilling pierced the silence. It was the women and girls, happy to be up and going out to the fields. After a cup of coffee and some bread, we too were all set for the harvest.

It was still barely light outside, and the air was sweet and cool. Ahead of us were the shadowy silhouettes of the women and girls, talking and singing, reed baskets slung on their backs. In the forest, some of the women were already tapping the trees to help the last ripe argans fall. The women began to gather them, squatting down, forming circles around the perimeter of the argan carpets, throwing the yellow and golden-brown fruit into baskets as they worked towards the tree trunk. I crouched beside the women, me in my practical blue jeans, they in their feminine tamelhafs, and together we worked, slowly filling the baskets. The woman beside me impaled a brown scorpion on a twig and brandished it in the air, inches from my nose.

I was finally face to face with one of my worst fears. "You would be sick, but not die from this one..." she told me.

The work went on until dozens of baskets were full to the brim. "It's a good year," Fatima said, to which the woman beside me chimed in: "There's no money here, just argans!" Although the women all laughed, I sensed a touch of despair and found myself hoping that if money came to Tafraoute it wouldn't spoil the harmony and integrity of their daily lives.

About ten o'clock, when the sun began to burn our backs, it was agreed that the gathering work was done for the day. Simon and I wished them all goodbye and then hitched a ride back to Tafraoute, where we strolled around the weekly souk. A group of women were sitting beside their wares: a dozen or so bottles of argan oil and amlou. A couple of storeowners displayed a few sacks of argan kernels; it wasn't exactly a roaring trade and my purchase of a half-litre each of oil and amlou attracted much attention.

That night, we were guests of the Caid again. He greeted our return not only with questions about our visit with Fatima, but with a surprise: he had arranged for us to be taken by another Caid to visit his region, a long drive south to Afilah Irghir, and we would leave early the following morning. One tree adventure was leading us to another.

For now, back on my comfortable divan at the Caidat, I thought of Fatima as I drifted to sleep, with visions of pink mountains and lush oases before my eyes.

LUNCH WITH THE SHEIKH

The Caid of Afilah Irghir sat next to me in the front seat, taciturn and rather stiff, when we set off southwards at seven o'clock the next morning. Typically Moroccan in build, neither tall nor heavy, he wore his black hair short and slicked down. He looked business-like in black spectacles and a tight-fitting brown suit, strangely out of place in his rustic surroundings.

The strip of paved road that leads south through the arid rose-colored ranges of the Anti Atlas Mountains, soon gave way to a tortuous rock-strewn piste. Dust churned up by the Land Rover's tires blew up in clouds and wafted through the windows, so I wound my Blue Man's turban around my hair and nostrils. Simon, lost to all human communication, was seeing everything through the eyes of his camera. He asked over and over for us to stop for photographs; requests borne patiently by both the Caid and the driver.

The piste took us on through jagged outcrops, sudden gorges and drowsy settlements built from the baked reddish-pink earth they stood on. It looked as if they had risen up out of the ground, untouched by human hand. The Caid was sitting quite silent, which I assumed meant he had important administrative things on his mind. I told him in Arabic how beautiful his country was, which seemed not only to confirm what he already knew, but pleased him to hear it said in his own language. After a while, perhaps in response to my enthusiasm, he began to soften and explain the things we were seeing. The stark fortress built on a mountain crest was where villagers kept grain and valuables safe. The wild orchards surrounding the settlements were filled with apricot, almond, pomegranate and fig trees, which, as well as a few goats, were the rural Berbers' only means of livelihood. The sole reminders of the twentieth century were the satellite dishes, battery-run, because electricity was still a distant prospect.

Further on, we came across a group of women gathered about a muddy village well. Wearing their glossy black tamelhafs, they were hard to miss in that biscuit-tinted land. As we approached, they stopped their work and we all stood staring for a moment, confronted by each other's strangeness. Brown-skinned children scampered barefoot in tattered shirts and dresses playing at games without toys, their eyes burning with curiosity as they watched us. Beside a group of mud houses stood a small cinder-block school hut, where hopefully their curiosity found encouragement. When Simon pointed to his camera, the women turned their faces aside. A young girl called out brazenly, "Arteni T-shirt!" She wanted to trade a photo for my T-shirt. From the beginning of our travels, we had decided not to give money or personal possessions for posed photographs. Our subjects would agree of their own free will or we would not shoot them, except from a distance. I shook my head and we all laughed as we drove off.

Some while later, we descended a jagged escarpment and came to a mosque the colour of copper, with turquoise-green roof tiles that glinted in the blinding mid-day sun. Beside it, a group of men were crouching in the shade of a spiny acacia. They watched, blankly, as we got out of the Land Rover and followed the Caid along a rutted path towards a sparse settlement that seemed forgotten by time. We were in Timgeguicht, site of one of the oldest mosques in Morocco.

We hadn't gone far when a tall, hefty old man with a saintly white beard and thick grey turban, appeared from the doorway of a simple square house and gave the Caid a rigid wave of his arm. I noticed first the curved silver dagger hanging to one side of his body, and the well-worn brown leather satchel on the other; and then the calloused heels that stuck out from a pair of scuffed babouches. As we neared the old man, he bowed to the Caid and ushered us into the house. We followed him up several flights of steep stone stairs, greatly relieved to find it cooler inside. Women and girls peeped at us from a kitchen door, giggling as we passed. At the top of the house, we turned into a small rectangular room.

Another man entered, and a wide smile of welcome lit his intelligent face when he saw the Caid. The man appeared to be in his fifties and, in spite of his faded grey robes and turban, radiated authority. We were in the house of the local Sheikh. After much protocol between the men – cheek kissing, repeated asking after the health of their families, and the thanking of Allah for his mercies – the Sheikh gestured for us to be seated. Two thin mattresses topped by a copious amount of cushions lay on the floor in one corner of the low-ceilinged room; the only other item of furniture was a low round table. The Caid introduced us and I offered the Sheikh my customary explanation about our book, at which he rubbed his hands together with satisfaction.

The old man, who appeared to be the Sheikh's valet, came into the room carrying a clay bowl containing warm newly baked bread, soft country butter and dark honey for dipping. To our surprise, while we ate, the valet, standing stock still, his huge frame towering above us, began to fan us with a huge palm frond to keep us cool and swish away any flies.

The bread was delicious; we were hungry and ate it all, forgetting that food always came in many courses. A few minutes later, the valet set a sizzling mutton tajine on the table together with more bread. The Sheikh pressed us to eat, tossing pieces of fatty meat to our side of the bowl. It was difficult to separate the fat from the lean in front of his eyes, but after making the pretence of chewing a lot, I sat back, hoping it would indicate I was full.

But the gesture went unnoticed. The valet soon returned with the obligatory couscous, and then went back to fanning us again. I was wondering about the women who had prepared this feast in such a short time; were they the Sheikh's wives, his daughters, maids, his neighbours? While I was receiving the same hospitality extended to a man, the women were in the kitchen.

When the meal was over, we'd been sitting and eating for two hours, and I was surprised to see the Sheikh perform the tea ceremony himself. He began by setting a huge kettle over a bed of burning charcoal. When it had boiled, he poured the water into a teapot packed with mint leaves and lump sugar and set it over the charcoal to brew. Soon the room filled with steam and a sweet minty aroma. By the time the Sheikh had filled our glasses three times, I felt like lying down on the mattress for a nap. Simon's eyes were drooping and the Caid, who had been smoking cigarettes and slowly falling lower and lower against the wall, suddenly got to his feet. He made his apologies to the Sheikh, saying we had to be at his Caidat before nightfall; the road was too difficult to find our way in the dark.

I left the Sheikh's house with mixed feelings: a warm glow from the unexpected and unreserved hospitality, and a heavy heart that was harder to explain.

BABA HALOU

I remember it was cold, the sky low with blustery grey rain clouds, when we arrived in Azrou that day in February. Azrou means rock in Berber, and there was a huge one on a hill at the edge of town, decorated with coloured bulbs and a metal crown like the roller-coaster on Coney Island, as if to drive home its significance.

We were making our way north, carrying with us all our baggage ready for departure to New York from Casablanca, so that when we got off the bus that had brought us from Marrakesh and looked around us, we felt like forlorn refugees who had made it to the wrong country. Our black bags and camera equipment looked entirely out of place against the rural rocky backdrop, and our fair features and blue eyes stood out like beacons beside the dusky complexions of the Berber farmers that milled about the bus terminus.

Colonel Jana had telephoned ahead on our behalf to one Baba Halou, Daddy Sweet, to ask him to kindly put us up for a few days while we went exploring the ancient cedar forests of the Middle Atlas. The Colonel and Baba Halou had once attended Azrou's famous Berber College together. But all we knew that day, as we stood there shivering, was that Baba Halou had a fabric stall in the town's Kisseriat, an indoor market.

Thirsty and disoriented, we ducked into a café in the small sloping town square that overlooked a vista of muddy-green hills. A cheery waiter brought us piping hot cups of creamy coffee, and we asked, "Where is the Kisseriat? Do you know Baba Halou?" He sounded like

143

someone that everyone in the small town would know, an institution. The waiter took us to the door and pointed down the mulberry tree-lined street towards a grey concrete building. "Baba Halou in there," he said.

He was standing behind a small wooden counter in a stall about twelve feet square, one among many set in rows inside the bare-bones building. The shelves behind him were lined with bolts of fabric, wools, linens, and synthetics in sober greys, browns and beiges. Other shops sold caftans, djellabas and burnooses, but the market was empty of customers as it was approaching the time for lunch. Everything and everyone stopped, everywhere, for the mid-day meal.

About sixty years old, Baba Halou's short hair, with its touch of distinguished gray at the temples, was topped by a cylindrical hat of brown fur, a bit like astrakhan, and the elegant hand-sewn wool djellaba he wore was finely striped in brown and beige. His brown eyes sparkled when we stopped in front of him and we stuttered, "Vous êtes Baba Halou?" "Oui, oui," he replied, and his face lit up as he stepped from behind the counter to shake our hands, which he did with great enthusiasm. "Vous êtes les amis américains de Colonel Jana," he said in perfect French. We both nodded, and smiled.

Baba Halou looked at his watch, closed the door to his stall and rubbed his hands together, as if in anticipation of something exciting, or maybe just because they were cold. "Nimshiu el dar," let's go home, he said. He insisted on pulling my suitcase on its wheels and led us briskly down the bumpy backstreets of town until we arrived at the wrought-iron gate of a two-story stone house, surrounded by a yard of cypress trees and evergreen shrubs.

Once inside the front door, Baba Halou marched briskly up a flight of stone stairs that took us into a large hallway with a polished stone floor. The warm smell of food struck us like an invisible wave; thick aromas of mutton, ginger and saffron, and of warm bread, brought saliva to my mouth. Simon and I looked at each other, raised eyebrows in our code that said all was well. All was very well.

And then the family appeared, in a crowd, from the kitchen and from a living-room at the far end of the hallway, drawn by Baba Halou's cheery announcement of our arrival.

Three young men, all in their twenties, surrounded us, and shook our hands with hearty "marhabas," "bienvenues," "amrehbas" and "welcomes" - speaking in four languages: Arabic, French, Berber and English. Two of the men were Baba Halou's sons, Hassan and Abdellah, the other was Mustapha, the son-in-law. They were all dressed in sweaters and jeans, like young men everywhere. A woman wearing a dark plum-colored taffeta caftan and a lacy black headscarf which she held over most of her face remained in the large kitchen, and made us a small nod and smile when Baba Halou introduced her as his wife. While she carried on stirring the contents of a big saucepan, the daughter, Meryam, a slight modern-looking young woman with short chestnut hair, moved from her mother's side and came eagerly to kiss us on both cheeks.

We all stood in a huddle of surprise and expectation until Baba Halou took charge. "Here are your rooms," he said, as he advanced along the hall and deposited our bags inside the doors. The rooms were small and meagerly furnished, and we knew we were taking them over from family members. "The bathroom," Baba Halou said, pointing to a door. And then everyone left us and drifted back to what they had been doing before our arrival.

We washed our hands, tidied up, and then found our way to the large living-room where the young men were sitting on divans arranged against the walls, a low round table set with plates and utensils before them. Their mid-day routine was being interrupted by our presence; they sat waiting, awkward, their conversation stiffened, until Baba Halou sat down with us and presided, the elder who brought wisdom and constancy to the table.

The room, indeed the whole house, was cold. There was clearly no heating of any sort. We were all wearing our sweaters, and I wondered if they felt the cold as much as I did. I forgot my shivering when Meryam brought circles of flat griddle bread, hot, filled with a spicy tomato and onion mixture, and placed them on the table. When Baba Halou pushed the bread towards me and I broke off a piece, trying not to show how famished I was. Hunger and food bring all peoples together. And bread is always a whetter of appetites. The men began to eat, at first politely and slowly. "Bnin," I said, very good, somehow managing to talk, chew and grin at the same time, all of which seemed to be the signal for everyone to tuck in.

The tajine we had smelled all this time came then to the table, carried in ceremoniously from the kitchen by the reclusive mother. Having given us her offering she promptly left again. I asked why. "She is going to pray," said Baba Halou. How extraordinary, I thought, to spend hours preparing a dish, present it to your family, and then leave the enjoyment of the dish and the company to go and pray. We knit into a circle around the steaming dish, all of us, using fingers and bread to eat, intent on devouring, but intent too on not taking more than our share. I had learned that satisfying one's hunger always depended on how many people were sharing and how copious the dish. In other words, if the meal was large, everyone was satisfied; if it was small, at least you were satisfied that you had shared what there was. A dish to oneself is the way we Westerners avoid this tricky issue. But there's something vital lost in not sharing, a sense of the importance of others, of the meeting and compromising of our needs with theirs.

I felt a bit warmer after the food, even warmer when Meryam brought in the pot of meal-ending mint tea and we drank two or three glasses of the hot sweet beverage. "Where do you want to go tomorrow?" Baba Halou asked. "My sons will show you the forests, whatever you want," he said. Hassan, with a glowing face and eyes, sat forward. "Yes, you must see le cèdre gouraud, the tallest and oldest," he said. "Eight hundred years old!"

Baba Halou left around three o'clock to go back to his business, Meryam disappeared to help her mother with the kitchen chores, and we were left with the young men who seemed not to have any occupation that called them away. It seemed the least I could do was to follow their custom, which meant leaving the men to their own company and going to help the women. I turned as I left the room, and saw Hassan move closer to Simon and put his arm around his shoulder with brotherly affection. I heard the others start to joke and laugh too, as I retreated from their world.

Before Baba Halou returned home that evening, I managed to take a nap in my borrowed bed, thawing out under thick wool blankets. The following day was the start of Ramadan - or would be, provided the new moon was sighted that night. The thought of fasting, considering the cold, seemed much more daunting than it had at other times. But we were here, and there was no way around Ramadan. That evening, a big tureen of harira soup was prepared in readiness for Ramadan's nightly fast-breaking, and some of it was served for supper. We sat afterwards under blankets, talking about our travels in their country until I couldn't keep my eyes open any longer and excused myself to go to bed.

The following morning, it was announced that Ramadan had begun. With great tolerance and forbearance, the mother made us some coffee and thick crêpes called msman, doused with warm butter and honey, which we ate as inconspicuously as possible in the living-room, stoking up for the long hours before breaking the fast at sunset. The young men came in and teased us. "Ha! You eat," they said. "And us? No, no, we're joking. Come, we've borrowed a car. Let's go."

The following days the young men showed us their countryside as if we were sightseeing a city. We drove through the dark cedar forest, stopping in damp undergrowth, in the company of skittish Barbary macaques, to crane our necks upwards hundreds of feet to the distant treetops that were like spires in a cathedral. We drove up from the tiny market village of Aïn Leuh to a bleak and scraggy plateau that reminded me of Scotland, and sat to rest on weirdly-shaped limestone rocks, beside an ancient loch called a dayat. We wound back down into muddy river valleys burgeoning with conifers and holly oak. We forgot, with our companions, thoughts of lunch filling our empty stomachs, and only returned to the house at sundown, to break the fast with the whole family: soup, dates, hard-boiled eggs, bread, followed by hot milky coffee.

Afterwards, we went out to visit their friends. The young men insisted that Simon wear a rough wool djellaba. "You don't look Moroccan," they joked, pulling the hood over his blond hair. "You still don't," they laughed. We spent hours playing cards - a complicated game they patiently taught us. On the way home, we stopped in town, transformed by lights and gaiety, all inhabitants abroad to share the evening's fasting reprieve. We ate donuts fried in great vats of boiling smoking oil, and chebekia cakes drowned in honey. Baba Halou remained at home with his wife and daughter, who all greeted our return and drew us into the living-room to talk about what we had done that day and evening. We brought things back from the stalls that were open all night: meat and vegetables for the late-night dinner, oranges and bananas.

I stayed up as long as I could into the night, even after Meryam and her mother had bid us goodnight. But when my eyes drooped beyond control, I left Simon with the men and made for my bed.

On the day we had planned to leave for Casablanca, we packed our bags. The young men sat silent in the living-room. Meryam brought us some bread and hard-boiled eggs for the journey, and the mother came from her kitchen and took my hand. When we were ready to leave, our big black bags at the top of the stairs, Baba Halou appeared in the hallway. As he shook our hands, he said, "Stay a few more days. Stay…" he repeated, looking deeply into my eyes. "We need you here."

The words were like arrows, piercing and sweet, like Baba Halou himself. It was a sobering and heartwarming thought that a family whose life we had so blithely interrupted, whose hospitality we had needed, could also need us.

LEAVING

I moved eight times during my seven years in Marrakesh, living the life of a seasoned nomad. But the moves were cathartic and kept my life free of possessions. For most of the moves, Meriam was the mistress of ceremonies, making my new home scrupulously clean and ready for a new phase in my life to begin. As soon as the house was cleaned, she would swiftly arrange my belongings, so that within a few hours it would seem I had been there for years.

The last of such moves augured the end of my prolonged sojourn in Marrakesh. When I had to leave the house I so loved in Arsat el Hamid, I went back to live in Gueliz, which held little appeal for me compared to the Medina. But it was a step towards the modern world that I sensed I was shortly to re-enter. It was a nice top-floor apartment in a somewhat rundown pink-washed art-deco villa rented by Michel, a French friend. Michel was gay, a debonair and intelligent man with sun-bleached blond hair, who had somehow survived eighteen years in Marrakesh, though he was much the poorer from an irrepressibly charitable disposition, and more world-weary, having a taste for Marrakesh's particular kind of night life, than when he had arrived. He was the only person with whom I could discuss politics and literature, and what it was about Marrakesh that kept foreigners like us captive so long. Even as I recognized why Michel doggedly refused to admit it was time to return to his country and family, I knew the end was in sight for me.

I finally found the courage to leave Morocco. At dawn, on a chill winter's day, coincidentally, Christmas Eve, I bundled myself into an old Mercedes. In a darkened alley in the still-sleeping Medina, I was driven by a man whose face I could barely see because of the deep wool hood of his burnoose, which had fallen over his brow. By the evening of that same day, I had climbed into a yellow cab outside the airport, and was being driven up the wide traffic-clogged avenues of New York City that were all aglow from the illuminated department store windows and a multitude of Christmas trees draped in lights.

When I left Morocco, I thought it was forever; I had to tell myself that. As the weeks and months passed, I would have dreams and visions of its startling red-earth landscapes, and memories of its vibrant people crowded in on me. The colours, scents and sensuality, the sun, the relentless heat, the light, the visible and invisible things of everyday life, everything was intact. I would never get my fill of these things, if I were to live in Morocco all my life.

A year later, I went back to visit. I stood in Djemaa el Fna, in the country I loved, beside the man I loved. "Your life here was a miracle," he said, shaking his head in disbelief, just as he had when we first met. Part of me belonged in Morocco and longed to live there again; the other part belonged at home with my family. All the things I experienced in Morocco are part of me now and have changed my life forever.

Morocco draws you to it, then intoxicates and holds you, but never yields itself fully. I had wanted to become Moroccan, thinking I would be privy then to all its secrets, but perhaps it does not yield its mystery fully, even to Moroccans.

eyeSight

Our greatest fear is not that we are inadequate, our greatest fear is that we are powerful beyond measure. By shining your light, you subconsciously give permission to others to shine theirs.
Nelson Mandela

Travel can be a liberating experience, as it was for me in 1990, when I was just one hundred yards from Nelson Mandela as he was released from prison. I watched this monumental occasion from on top of a traffic light, amidst a sea of enthralled onlookers.

This was the 'green light' moment that inspired the creation of Eye Books. From the chaos of that day arose an appreciation of the opportunities that the world around us offers, and the desire within me to shine a light for those whose reaction to opportunity is 'can't and don't'.

Our world has been built on dreams, but the drive is often diluted by the corporate and commercial interests offering to live those dreams for us, through celebrity culture and the increasing mechanisation and automation of our lives. Inspiration comes now from those who live outside our daily routines, from those who *challenge the way we see things*.

Eye Books was born to tell the stories of *'ordinary' people doing 'extraordinary' things*. With no experience of publishing, or the constraints that the book 'industry' imposes, Eye Books created a genre of publishing to champion those who live out their dreams.

Twelve years on, and sixty plus stories later, Eye Books has the same ethos. We believe that ethical publishing matters. It is not about just trying to make a quick hit, it is about publishing the stories that affect our lives and the lives of others positively. We publish the books we believe will shine a light on the lives of some and enlighten the lives of many for years to come.

Join us in the Eye Books community, and share the power these stories evoke.

Dan Hiscocks
Founder and Publisher
Eye Books

www.eye-books.com

At Eye Books we are constantly challenging the way we see things and do things. But we cannot do this alone. To that end we have created an online club, a community, where members can inspire and be inspired, share knowledge and exchange ideas. Membership is free, and you can join by visiting www.eye-books.com, where you will be able to find:

What we publish
Books that truly inspire, by people who have given their all, triumphed over adversity, lived their lives to the full. Visit the dedicated microsites we have for each of our books online.

Why we publish
To champion those 'ordinary' people doing extraordinary things. The real celebrities of our world who tell stories that celebrate life to the full, not just for 15 minutes. Books where fact is more compelling than fiction.

How we publish
Eye Books is committed to ethical publishing. Many of our books feature and campaign for various good causes and charities. We try to minimise our carbon footprint in the manufacturing and distribution of our books.

Who we publish
Many, indeed most of our authors have never written a book before. Many start as readers and club members. If you feel strongly that you have a book in you, and it is a book that is experience driven, inspirational and life affirming, visit the 'How to Become an Author' page on our website. We are always open to new authors.

Eye-Books.com Club is an ever-evolving community, as it should be, and benefits from all that our members contribute, with invitations to book launches, signings and author talks, plus special offers and discounts on the books we publish.

Eye Books membership is free, and it's easy to sign up. Visit our website. Registration takes less than a minute.

eyeBookshelf

THE AMERICAS / ASIA

Category	Thunder & Sunshine — Alastair Humphreys	The Good Life — Dorian Amos	The Good Life Gets Better — Dorian Amos	Cry From the Highest Mountain — Tess Burrows	Riding the Outlaw Trail — Simon Casson & Richard Adamson	Trail of Visions Route 2 — Vicki Couchman	Riding with Ghosts — Gwen Maka	Riding with Ghosts – South of the Border — Gwen Maka	Lost Lands Forgotten Stories — Alexandra Pratt	Frigid Women — Sue & Victoria Riches	Touching Tibet — Niema Ash	First Contact — Mark Anstice	Tea for Two — Polly Benge	Baghdad Business School — Heyrick Bond Gunning
eyeThinker		•	•	•		•		•	•		•	•	•	•
eyeAdventurer	•	•	•		•		•	•	•	•		•	•	•
eyeQuirky				•										
eyeCyclist	•						•	•					•	
eyeRambler														
eyeGift	•			•										
eyeSpiritual														

THE AMERICAS (Thunder & Sunshine … Touching Tibet) — **ASIA** (First Contact, Tea for Two, Baghdad Business School)

AFRICA / EUROPE

Category	Moods of Future Joys — Alastair Humphreys	Green Oranges on Lion Mountain — Emily Joy	Zohra's Ladder — Pamela Windo	Walking Away — Charlotte Metcalf	Changing the World from the inside out — Michael Meegan	All Will Be Well — Michael Meegan	Seeking Sanctuary — Hilda Reilly	Crap Cycle Lanes — Captain Crunchynutz	50 Quirky Bike Rides…in England and Wales — Rob Ainsley	On the Wall with Hadrian — Bob Bibby	Special Offa — Bob Bibby	The European Job — Jonathan Booth	Fateful Beauty — Natalie Hodgson	Slow Winter — Alex Hickman
eyeThinker		•	•	•	•	•								•
eyeAdventurer	•	•						•				•	•	•
eyeQuirky								•	•					
eyeCyclist	•							•	•					
eyeRambler										•	•			
eyeGift	•						•							
eyeSpiritual					•		•							

AFRICA (Moods of Future Joys … Seeking Sanctuary) — **EUROPE** (Crap Cycle Lanes … Slow Winter)

eyeBookshelf

ASIA / AUS

Book	eyeThinker	eyeAdventurer	eyeQuirky	eyeCyclist	eyeRambler	eyeGift	eyeSpiritual
Jungle Janes — Peter Burden		•					
Trail of Visions — Vicki Couchman	•	•				•	
Desert Governess — Phyllis Ellis	•		•				
Fever Tress of Borneo — Mark Eveleigh		•					
My Journey with a Remarkable Tree — Ken Finn	•						
The Jungle Beat — Roy Follows	•	•					
Siberian Dreams — Andy Home	•	•					
Behind the Veil — Lydia Laube		•					
Good Morning Afghanistan — Waseem Mahmood	•	•					
Jasmine and Arnica — Nicola Naylor	•						
Prickly Pears of Palestine — Hilda Reilly	•						
Last of the Nomads — W J Peasley	•	•					
Travels in Outback Australia — Andrew Stevenson	•						

EUROPE / CROSS CONTINENT

Book	eyeThinker	eyeAdventurer	eyeQuirky	eyeCyclist	eyeRambler	eyeGift	eyeSpiritual
The Accidental Optimist's Guide to Life — Emily Joy	•		•				
Con Artist Handbook — Joel Levy	•		•			•	
Forensics Handbook — Pete Moore	•	•	•			•	
Travels with my Daughter — Niema Ash	•	•	•				
Around the World with 1000 Birds — Russell Boyman							
Death — Herbie Brennan	•	•		•		•	•
Discovery Road — Tim Garratt & Andy Brown	•		•				
Great Sects — Adam Hume Kelly	•						
Triumph Around the World — Robbie Marshall		•					
Blood Sweat and Charity — Nick Stanhope		•					
Traveller's Tales from Heaven and Hell — Various			•			•	
Further Traveller's Tales from Heaven and Hell — Various			•			•	
More Traveller's Tales from Heaven and Hell — Various			•			•	

Riding with Ghosts
Gwen Maka
£7.99

Gwen Maka, a forty-something Englishwoman, was told by everyone that her dream of cycling from Seattle to Costa Rica, across the deserts, over the Rocky Mountains, and into the sub-tropics of Central America, was impossible.

Riding with Ghosts is Gwen's frank but never too serious account of her epic 7,500 mile cycling tour. She handles exhaustion, climatic extremes, lechers and a permanently saddle-sore bum in a gutsy, hilarious way. Her journey, intertwined with the legends of past events, is a testimony to the power of determination.

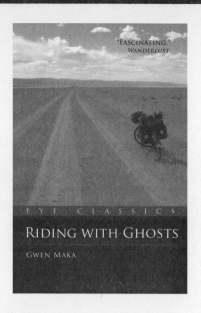

Frigid Women
Sue & Victoria Riches
£7.99

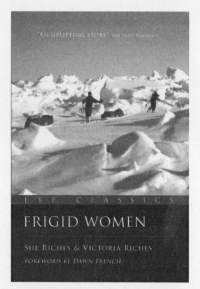

Women wanted to walk to North Pole, the advert read. Sue & Victoria Riches, mother and daughter, never imagined how much one small article in a newspaper would change their lives.... Within two years, they were trekking across the frozen wilderness that is the Arctic Ocean, as part of the first all women's expedition to the North Pole. At times totally terrifying and at times indescribably beautiful, it was a trip of a lifetime. Having survived cancer treatment and a mastectomy it was an opportunity to discover that *anything* is possible if you put your mind to it.

www.eye-books.com

Riding the Outlaw Trail
Simon Casson
£7.99

A dramatic account of what it was like
following the trail of the most elusive
and successful bandits of the Wild West:
Butch Cassidy and the Sundance Kid.
An obsessive trouble-shooter and a
cool-thinking, ex-Special Forces Marine
Commando, with nothing in common
but mutual suspicion, join forces for a
gruelling, hazardous 5-month horseback
journey across 2,000 miles of desert,
mountain, canyon & high-plains
wilderness through the 'Old West'.

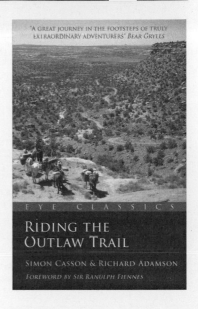

Triumph Around the World
Robbie Marshall
£7.99

At 45 Robbie Marshall had it all, or so
it seemed. So what on earth made him
trade his suit for leathers, his office for
the saddle of a great British motorcycle,
and his bulging appointments diary for an
out-of-date world atlas?

The prospect of a new challenge held
such overwhelming appeal that he was
prepared to risk it all – his hard-won
career, wealth and the love of a good
woman – for life on the road, and a life-
style completely removed from anything
he had known before.

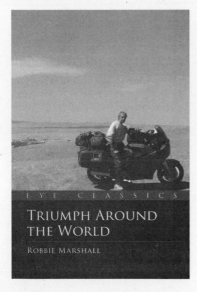

www.eye-books.com

Jasmine & Arnica
Nicola Naylor
£7.99

Nicola Naylor had always been enthralled by India, but her travel fantasies dissolved when she lost her sight. Overcoming her own private fears and disregarding the warnings, Naylor set out to experience India alone.

This is the inspiring account of her unique journey. Told with a vivid and evocative insight, *Jasmine & Arnica* is a story of a young woman's determination, a celebration of the power of vision, beyond sight, to reveal what's closest to the heart, and to uncover life's most precious, unseen joys.

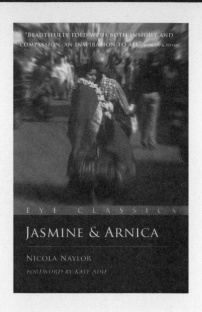

Touching Tibet
Niema Ash
£7.99

Niema Ash was one of the first people to enter Tibet when its borders were briefly opened to Westerners in 1986. In this highly absorbing and personal account, she relates with wit, compassion and sensitivity her encounters with people whose humour, spirituality and sheer enthusiasm for life have carried them through years of oppression and suffering.

Touching Tibet takes the reader on a unique journey into the heart of this intriguing forbidden kingdom.

www.eye-books.com

eyeAuthor

Pamela Windo

Pam Windo was born in Brighton. She left school to travel to Paris and Berlin, then to North Africa where she lived with a young Tunisian and his family, and worked as radio operator on a dam-building site. Back in England, after a first marriage and divorce, and now mother of two boys, she hooked up with childhood friend Gary Windo, a gifted saxophone player. In London, she found herself jamming, gigging and recording with musicians like Nick Mason of Pink Floyd and Robert Wyatt of Soft Machine.

When Pam immigrated with Gary to Woodstock, New York, she started her own band "Pam Windo & the Shades" and was signed by music mogul Albert Grossman. In the mid-1980s, she escaped the music business and went to live in Marrakesh. She lived there for seven years, teaching English, writing for magazines, and working on Martin Scorsese's movie, *Kundun*, shot entirely in Morocco. In 2004, a retrospective CD of Gary and Pam's music was released and chosen by the BBC as their "Album of the Week."

What inspired you to write your book?
I first went to Morocco for a three-month escape from city life and found it intoxicating; Morocco is an incredibly beautiful and unspoiled country. My travels and experiences with the people everywhere were so fascinating and enriching that I couldn't help but write it all down.

How would you describe your books?
Books that attempt to connect intimately with the reader, in sharing as honestly as possible the passionate moments and experiences of my life in Morocco.

What do you hope readers will get from your books?
That they will relate to the experiences I describe, and will either get up and go too, or simply enjoy and learn from the experience through my eyes.

Which writers do you admire?
A book either grabs me or it doesn't, whether the author is famous or not. There are so many I can't list them all, but amongst the authors I love are Colette, Anaïs Nin, Gide, Camus, E.M. Forster, Graham Greene and Jean Rhys.

Which books have influenced you?
All of the above, but in particular Colette, as she was so daring and individual.

www.eye-books.com